GW00691300

SYRIA
LAND OF CONTRASTS

SYRIA
LAND OF CONTRASTS

PETER LEWIS
PHOTOGRAPHS BY ROBIN CONSTABLE

NAMARA PUBLICATIONS

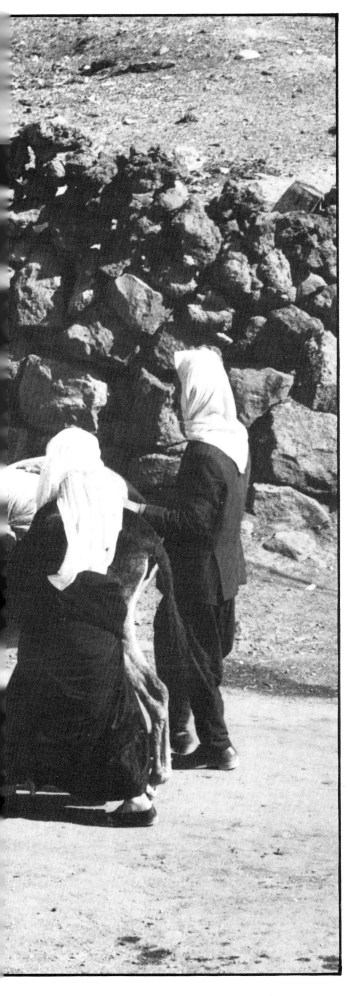

Contents

First published by Namara Publications
Limited 1980
A member of the Namara Group
45/46 Poland Street, London W1

ISBN 0 7043 2220 X

Designed by Namara Features Limited

Printed in Great Britain by
E. J. Arnold & Son Limited, Leeds

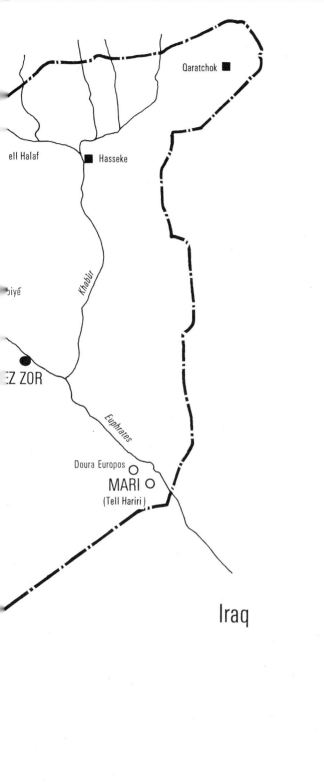

Qaratchok ■

ell Halaf   ■ Hasseke

Khabūr

biyé

EZ ZOR ●

Euphrates

Doura Europos ○
MARI ○
(Tell Hariri)

Iraq

Syria

```
      50           100 km
```

○ Places of Historical Interest
■ Towns

Acknowledgements

We would like to acknowledge the courtesy of the Minister of Information, Mr Ahmed Iskandar Ahmed, in entertaining us and arranging hospitality on our journeys and also the help of Mr Zuheir Jannan, of the Ministry of Information, Dr Afif Bahnassi, Director General of Antiquities and Museums, Dr Kassem Toueir, of the National Museum, Damascus, Dr Khaled Assad, Director of Antiquities at Palmyra, and Professor Paolo Matthiae, of the University of Rome, the discoverer of Ebla. We also thank our friend and guide, Mr Costandi Hamati.

CHRONOLOGY
of Main Events

BC
- *c.* 2700 Kingdoms of Mari and Ebla in being
- 2400 Mari conquered by Ebla
- 2250 Ebla destroyed by Naram-Sin, king of Akkad
- 1750 Mari destroyed by Hammurabi, king of Babylon
- 1468 Damascus conquered by Tuthmoses III of Egypt
- *c.* 1400 First alphabet invented in city-kingdom of Ugarit
- *c.* 1200 Ugarit destroyed by the 'People of the Sea'
- 732 Damascus conquered by the Assyrian king, Tiglath-Pileser
- 572 Babylonian conquest by Nebuchadnezzar
- 538 Persian conquest of Syria by Cyrus the Great
- 333 Alexander the Great conquers Syria and the Persian Empire
- 312 Seleucus, Alexander's successor, rules Syria
- 169 Nabatean kingdom of Petra rules southern Syria and, later, Damascus
- 64 Pompey annexes·Syria to the Roman Empire

AD
- *c.* 31–4 St Paul at Damascus, then at Antioch
- 244–9 A Syrian, Philip the Arab, becomes Emperor of Rome
- 262 Odenathus of Palmyra defeats the Persians and is proclaimed commander of the eastern Roman Empire
- 271 Queen Zenobia, his widow, declares Palmyra's independence and is taken captive to Rome in 274
- 395 Division of Roman Empire. Syria ruled by Constantinople
- *c.* 590 The Prophet Muhammad visits Syria as a young man
- 630 Muhammad leads armed expedition from Arabia to Syrian border
- 634–6 Muslim conquest of Syria
- 661 Omayyad dynasty of Caliphs founded in Damascus. Muslim empire extended from the Indus valley to Spain
- 705–15 Building of the Great Mosque at Damascus by Caliph Walid
- 750 Fall of the Omayyads: rise of the Abbasid Caliphs at Baghdad
- 1096 The Crusades are launched. Jerusalem captured, 1099. Damascus withstands repeated sieges
- 1187 Saladin, ruler of Damascus, recaptures Jerusalem
- 1271 The greatest Crusader castle, Krak des Chevaliers, falls to Sultan Beybars
- 1299 Mongol invasion of Syria
- 1400 Tamerlane and the Mongols devastate Damascus and Aleppo
- 1516 Ottoman Turks occupy Syria
- 1918 Liberation from the Turks by Arab and British troops
- 1920 French mandate over Syria
- 1946 Syria independent
- 1970 President Assad inaugurates new government and constitution

The sherbet seller's gleaming armour

DAMASCUS

D AMASCUS . . . dust-brown city half as old as Time. Older yet than rose-red Petra, of which this was written, and which crumbled into dust while Damascus was still in its youth. The three evocative syllables of its name act like a drug on the imagination, conjuring visions of silks and swords, camel trains and Caliphs and carpets, bazaars and brocades and beggars, roses and Roman arches, minarets and mosaics, murky passageways and mystery.

It is the oldest inhabited capital city in the world, dating back to the third millennium before Christ, even to before Abraham, according to Genesis. In its time it has been capital of its own Aramean kingdom under pagan gods, then of a Roman province under Jupiter, then the first headquarters of St Paul and a principal centre of the early Christians, then the capital of Islam, seat of the Caliphs of an empire stretching from Spain to the borders of China. It was the centre of the Ottoman empire in the Levant when T. E. Lawrence climbed the heights overlooking the city on the night of 30 September 1918 to look at the long-sought prize awaiting the armies of General Allenby and Prince Faisal, which were to end the Turkish dominion the next day. 'We drove to the head of a ridge which stood over the oasis of the city, afraid to look North for the ruins we expected. But instead of ruins, the silent gardens stood blurred green with river mist, in whose setting shimmered the city, beautiful as ever, like a pearl in the morning sun.'

Lawrence's dreams of an Arab kingdom stretching from the Mediterranean to the Red Sea were dissolved in the bargaining at Paris. Damascus became a captive city again for a further thirty years until another world war brought independence back to Syria after nearly a thousand years. Highly unstable at first – there were twenty-three changes of government in twenty-four years – it has now achieved equilibrium. The Syrian republic, since 1970 under President Hafez al-Assad, is in the process of pulling itself up by its bootstraps economically – no small feat because two-thirds of the country is desert. Damascus once more enjoys the proud status it asserted so long ago in this racial and religious melting-pot between the Mediterranean and Mesopotamia.

Damascus wears all this history on her back like layers of coats on an ancient gipsy woman who has known luxury and poverty, power and servitude, absorbed it all and never thrown any shred of experience away. You will not see all these layers when you arrive. They have to be peeled away with patience and learning, like the levels of the ancient towns that lie buried under the Tells of the Syrian desert. The difference between Damascus and an archaeological site is that its people are still there, living noisily, hectically, chaotically among the ruins of their past and the emerging shape of their future. The first impression the city gives today is of a mesmerizing mixture of ancient and modern, made frantic by possibly the biggest traffic free-for-all in the Middle East. The western approach to the city is Westernized. A broad, tree-lined, dual-carriageway, the *Choukry al-Kouwatly*, advances into town between the international-style hotels, the government buildings and the exhibition halls and elongated star symbol of the International Trade Fair. The eastern end is the old city, almost unchanged behind its crumbling walls. But the centre, which is being completely reconstructed, is an adventure playground of fly-overs, dust, piles of cement and rubble, full of empty shells of concrete blocks swathed in trailing cable and half-lighted neon signs. It looks as though it will never be finished – for the Arabs, it must be said, have never been fanatical about tidying up – but the half-paved sidewalks and the yet unplanted banks and islands are already occupied by the street stalls, the shoe-shine men, the vendors of everything from sticky cakes to cacophonous tapes whose music howls above the traffic. Amid this concrete confusion the Arabs exercise their talent for creating hubbub. Every Arab driver believes it is his right to proceed directly where he wants to go the minute he thinks of it; provided he announces his intention with a hand on the horn, other road users have had all the warning they need expect. Exactly the same principle applies to pedestrians, mules and donkeys, although they have not the advantage of horns. The streets are a daily miracle of hair's-breadth escapes from certain death by blind providence. There are traffic lights but the stranger must learn which of them are disregarded by unspoken agreement. There are pedestrian crossings but he must learn to assume that the most notice that will be taken of them is for the traffic to slow down slightly, if enough people are crossing, before ploughing through their ranks. As for bicycles, which are numerous, they are, as a rule, ridden on the wrong side of the road in the wrong direction, without lights and with at least two people on them. Any traffic system can work if everyone knows what to expect and so does this – though the result is Babel.

If you want to experience the clash of centuries at its most dramatic, walk into the centre of the old city. You walk through the central aisle of the *suq*, that cathedral of salesmanship, and at its farthest end emerge under the open sky. You find yourself in a Roman colonnade, the capitals of the columns crusted with Corinthian acanthus leaves, their bases plunged into a clutter of stalls selling books, beads, perfume and holy trinkets. At one end they support the giant broken pediment of the Temple of Jupiter, the chief shrine of the Roman city, a massive ruin that Rome would be proud to own. Looking through the columns to the open sky you see framed between them the minarets of the Great Mosque built by the Omayyads, the dynasty of Caliphs of Damascus. A few yards further on stands its great gate and courtyard and at the farther end of the mosque you will see the faithful on their knees before the marble shrine to John the Baptist, where his severed head is believed to lie. So here, within 200 yards of each other, stand three temples representing three civilizations, three religions, three eras of man's history. Buried beneath them is an even older era. Just as the Great Mosque is built on and among the remains of the Christian basilica of St John the Baptist, so the Temple of Jupiter was built on the site of the god of thunder, Haddad, whom the Arameans worshipped here more than a thousand years before Christ. Each religion has built on the remains of its predecessor. This strip of ground at the heart of Damascus is indeed one of the longest established holy places on earth.

Almost every visitor to modern Damascus makes straight for the *suq* as countless generations have done before him. Its main covered way, the *Suq al-Hamadieh*, looms up like a Victorian railway station with its high, black, rusty corrugated iron roof, which lets in the sun one beam at a time through innumerable holes. Its entrance is besieged with taxis, money-changers and touts eagerly soliciting strangers, especially Europeans, to come with them to see their exceptional treasure house: 'You are English? Come and see my shop.

The cassette seller

Nuts in luscious profusion

Very nice things. Just look, not buy. See my wonderful show. Look today, buy tomorrow.' But you do not know where to look first, up or down. Because of the narrowness of their frontages, the merchants hang their goods high over the walls lining the pathway, like banners in a knights' chapel. The old stonework is caparisoned with cascades of carpets and kaftans, shoes and scarves, belts and baubles, bridal gowns and plastic bowls, colour and confusion, while the pathway itself is strewn with humbler objects. At first it leaves you stunned. There are twenty-six side alleys and some are devoted more or less exclusively to a trade – carpenters and cabinet makers or luggage and leather goods. But most of it is a blinding jumble of incongruities, antiques and cooking implements, table-cloths and tea-towels, inlaid wood and gaudy plastic, sombre Bedouin embroidery and brash cotton prints, the traditional and the atrocious cheek by jowl. The eye has to adjust from moment to moment from the best of the old East to the worst of the modern West. Here is an emporium glowing with burnished and chased brass-work, lit by lamps in coloured red and blue glass twinkling like a dream of Aladdin's. Here, a few feet away, is a blaze of the most vulgar chrome and gimcrack light fittings devised by modern man. Here are the most exquisite cabinets and chess-boards of inlaid wood and bone. There is a cluster of rainbow-dyed feather boas, like a flock of crazed ostriches. Here, in a patch of sunshine in a side alley, carpets are being rolled out on the ground to glow with the harmonies of Tabriz or Turkestan. Here are tapestries of the most hideous hues in which, say, an Arab boy is depicted with a tear running down his cheek in raw and shiny threads. Row upon row of deep crimson velvet kaftans encrusted with gold and rhinestones make one wonder if the *suq* has been ordered to costume a thousand Gertrudes for an endless production of *Hamlet*. Yet alongside them are western window dummies wearing western mass-produced dresses under western lacquered blonde

nylon wigs. And here about your feet are the mundane odds and ends of life sold straight off the footway itself. Here you will find a company of wooden coat-hangers ranged like soldiers in perfect dressing, another line of scarlet plastic Santa Clauses like puffy, poisonous toadstools, or a flashing array of electro-plated tea-trays or cake-stands each being polished by a solemn small boy with a cloth. You never know what you will trip over next but, however unpromising it may seem, it is somebody's livelihood and stock-in-trade.

Over all this flows the tide of shoppers, the cosmopolitan throng of the Oxford Street of the Levant wearing head-dresses of every kind – the Syrian *keffiyeh* in red-and-white or black-and-white check, the pure white Saudi head-dress, the white lacy skullcaps of serious old men, the black veils of women completely obscuring the face, the flash of metal headbands, of a row of gold discs or chain mail. A clink and clash as of cymbals announces the passage of the sherbet seller, a silver urn harnessed to his back like a segment of new moon, as he clashes his two brass cups together to attract custom and cries out 'Refresh your heart!' There is the splutter of a three-wheeled motor cart forcing its way through the crowd, the prodding of a patient donkey or the sour horn-blast of a Ministry Mercedes – the only cars allowed are official ones or the army vehicles which burst forth from the Citadel buried in the depths of the market.

It is the incongruities that most take the eye. The sight of a gold merchant weighing a bracelet on an antique pair of scales with their tiny round weights and then whipping out a pocket calculator to compute its value. The glimpse of a Saudi in full, spotless white robe holding up a frilly pink party dress on its hanger to check its size against his little daughter. There are ice cream parlours ablaze with neon and a sudden break in the Arabic shop signs to announce 'Max Factor'. Only a few yards away oriental perfume sellers market attar of roses, the crushed essences of rose petals, jas-

Spread out for judgment

Still-life with tea-pot

archways and balconies supported by the remains of barley-sugar columns and doorways carved with old Islamic decorative motifs for some vanished pasha. The sales techniques of the salesmen who speak English are an entertainment in themselves. Victor, of the Good Luck Stores, for instance, addresses you in a convent-learned English with surprising traces of a Birmingham accent and of outmoded army slang picked up from his many customers who passed by in the Second World War – often buying on tick but never failing, he tells you proudly, to pay up in army postal orders from all over the Middle East.

'Good evening, gentlemen,' he will begin. 'You like a shufti inside my shop? Come on in. Have a dekko. In other shops they would ask you 200 *lira* [Syrian pounds] for this item. I only ask 150 – small profit, quick return. This ring? Others would tell you ivory. It is bone, camel bone, I cannot tell a lie. You are broke? You will not have enough left to eat? But what is eating? You can eat every day. Tomorrow – phfft! It is gone. But this cloth you will have for years.'

Of course, the price is always an unheard-of bargain. You would never obtain it anywhere in the *suq* for goods of such quality. Of course, you are only being offered such an opportunity because the salesman has seen you are so tempted by it, he cannot disappoint you, he considers you as his own brother. Of course, there is no hurry – you would prefer tea or coffee while you think about it? Meanwhile he finds . . . ah, this, the very thing you have been looking for for your wife, sweetheart, mother, sister and – see – he will even include this box, this printed picture, this ashtray or antique ring absolutely free and for nothing when you make the purchase. Sit here and he will show you photographs of his family, of his European customers who are his friends, of his girl friend in Germany – 'very nice in the bed, very funny'. You must sign his visitors' book. You really have to go now?

mine, gardenia and orange blossom from a stall crowded with ancient, dusky bottles. And there are always the importunities of touts urging you to buy, buy, buy. Those in the street itself are often working for a merchant with a shop on the upper storey of the arcades which would otherwise be missed and therefore have to busk all the harder. Sometimes they will lead you up hidden stairways of stone steps worn into semi-circles by climbing feet since the Romans built them. Often the best articles are to be found upstairs or through a maze of side alleys leading to shut-away courtyards where ragged vines straggle and struggle to survive and there you may come upon old

Tradition lives on in the street scenes of Damascus

Students at the bus stop

The Temple of Jupiter wired for trading

Then, just a moment, there could be an adjustment in the price though by now, Allah knows, he is making no profit at all, he is giving it away for what he paid for it, even less, because he knows you want it so badly. He may even tell you, in a moment of astonishing frankness, that you are his only customer so far today and you must buy to bring him good luck and to make it a happy day and he will drink your health in whisky tonight. Scottish whisky. Indeed, tonight, why should you not drink whisky together and perhaps see some belly-dancing? It is not just a sale that is being brought to fruition, it is a personal bond – for as long as the transaction lasts at any rate. For those who are in a hurry, or who do not enjoy the parries and feints of bargaining, the *suq* is no place to go. What pleasure is there in a bald sale, without the time-honoured, time-consuming ritual? And what better way is there to spend time other than in bargaining on this spot which has been dedicated to it for so many centuries of haggling?

There *are* bargains – the best of them, naturally, being the products for which Damascus is famed. The brocades, the Bedouin-embroidered dresses, the bone-inlaid tables and chests and stools, the brass and copper engraved and inlaid with silver, the goldsmithery, the coins bearing Roman and Byzantine emperors' heads, the Roman glass, still crusted with desert dust but glowing with blue and violet lights where it has remained clear. But it behoves you to look carefully. There is a lot of clumsy or mass-produced work, masquerading as craftsmanship, produced for the undiscerning tourist in careless imitation of the old Damascene designs. A general rule with metal-work is the older, the better. In earlier eras men took more time over their work.

To step out of the hubbub of the *suqs* into the tranquillity of the Great Mosque is one of the most vivid contrasts to be experienced in Syria. The Omayyad Mosque lies in the centre of the markets like a huge boulder, untouched by the buffets of the surrounding sea. It is one of the greatest masterpieces of Islamic architecture and ranks fourth among the holy places of Islam – after Mecca, Medina and the Dome of the Rock in Jerusalem. The Omayyads were the dynasty which ruled over Islam for 100 years during the amazingly swift conquests which brought first the whole Middle East and then the whole of the North African coastland under their sway. The Omayya were one of the aristocratic families of Mecca and Othman was one of the first converts of the Prophet when he began to preach there around the year 613 AD. Certainly he was the first Meccan of high social standing to join Muhammad. He enjoyed his friendship and married two of the Prophet's daughters. He became Caliph in his sixties – the third of the Successors (Caliph means 'Successor') to Muhammad.

Carpet sellers use the railings for display

19

The prayer wall, Great Mosque

Thus began the Omayyad dynasty of Caliphs – the murder of Othman in 656 was one of the fateful turning points in the history of Islam and will be treated in a later chapter. His successors chose Damascus as their capital and it became the increasingly luxurious centre of their growing empire. By the time Caliph Walid succeeded in 705, Spain was ready to fall to the Muslim armies in the West and the Persian empire followed in the East, taking the rule of Damascus right across the river Indus in what is modern Pakistan and up to the borders of the Tang emperors of China. Walid's reign saw these conquests but he himself was more concerned with the building of the Great Mosque, his most enduring memorial. Its construction by Walid is recorded on a plaque beside the great gate, which is always open. He seized the church of St John the Baptist from the Christians and demolished most of it to make room for the mosque. He summoned thousands of craftsmen, many of them Christians from Constantinople, to beautify it. He collected lead from all over his empire to make the roof, and ships were summoned to bring gold and silver to decorate its columns and provide its mosaics. When he was criticized for his extravagance, according to Muslim tradition, he emptied the whole of his treasury into the building in a massive heap of gold and silver. In the end it cost him seven years of the empire's revenues but when the accounts came in he refused to read them, saying 'we have spent this for God and we will not count it'.

Through the open doors you can see the carpeted calm of the Mosque from the *suqs* and the bustle of the *suqs* from the Mosque's great oasis of a courtyard. Yet the two never seem to disturb one another. You leave worldly stress at the doorway, along with your shoes. Non-Muslims are not allowed to enter through the main gateway with its huge embossed bronze doors – they must use a side entrance just along the wall to the

left – but it is worth standing outside, especially on Friday, the Muslim Sabbath, to watch the tide of the faithful stepping over the raised sill, removing their boots or slippers all in one movement with scarcely a pause.

Inside the great gates, the first impression is almost one of having stepped into Venice. The vast, cool, finely proportioned courtyard feels as big as St Mark's Square after the narrowness of the *suqs* – but, like that miraculous piazza, it keeps the intimacy of a light, airy room. The mosaics high above your head glitter duskily with gold. The big, square-cut columns are patterned in geometric bas-relief. Along one of the long sides of the courtyard runs the outer wall of the prayer hall, inlaid with marble panels of delicately faded pinks and ochres. The remaining three sides are cloisters supported on slightly horseshoe shaped, nipped arches and surmounted by a clerestory of small, plain Roman arches. Even the spandrels and soffits of the arches are gilded with mosaic – at least, enough of it has survived to make you wonder at the original richness they must have presented in their early centuries. Soaring above the Mosque are its three minarets – two at the outer corners of the prayer hall, only visible from the streets outside. These two are known as the minaret of Sultan Qait Bey (the one you can see as you approach the main doors through the columns of the Roman Temple of Jupiter) and the minaret of Jesus. If it seems surprising that both Jesus and John the Baptist should be commemorated in one of the chief Muslim shrines, that is because the Christian world is widely ignorant of the extent to which both are honoured in the Koran. One Muslim tradition is that Jesus at the Second Coming will alight on the top of the minaret named after him. But the minaret that towers above the courtyard itself, the minaret of the Bride, though not the most beautiful, is the most extraordinary structure – a towering pinnacle of galleries, balconies and verandas, piled on top of each other nearly to the height of the shining globe on top. These are for delivering the call to prayer – though they are only used on the great feast days of the Islamic calendar. On ordinary days the *muezzin*'s voice floats out over the city from a recording played from loudspeakers attached to the minaret. With permission, you may climb up there – and reflect that perhaps the number of stairs to mount five times a day has proved too daunting for modern times. It is only from there that the onion-shaped central dome of the Mosque can be properly seen, the 'Dome of the Eagle'.

One of the chief glories of the Great Mosque is the richness of the mosaic decoration on the outer walls and around the courtyard:

a luxuriant townscape of palaces and classical buildings, emerging from a forest of glossy green trees against a background of blazing gold. It is like the Garden of Eden with buildings, which is probably how the Caliph's craftsmen thought of Damascus, which some say it represents. There are glimpses of rivers and bridges but it is empty both of people and animals, whose depiction is forbidden in Islam. Even in religious films about the Prophet, his face and form are never seen – only his feet. The only birds that fly about these trees are the live pigeons which perch along the pediment above it.

Earthquake, fire and conquest prevent us from seeing this marvellous decoration in its full glory. The first fire occurred in 1069. In 1400 Tamerlane burnt the Mosque with 30,000 men, women and children shut up inside it. Most of what we see was carefully reconstructed and redecorated after the disastrous fire of 1893 on the original model. But the gem of the courtyard is unaltered. It is the little domed octagon supported above ground on stubby Corinthian columns which stands all alone at one end of the square, each of its sides a rich and beautiful panel of pictorial mosaic – a little gallery of Islamic art at its oldest and finest. This was the treasury of the Mosque, its wealth stored high above the heads of anyone tempted to steal from it.

One of the surprises to the Western visitor used to the supervised hush of cathedrals is the casual way in which Muslims use their Great Mosque as a meeting place, a place to go for a chat, a rest in the shadows or somewhere to lie down and sleep. Children play in the courtyard and a cripple on a wheeled board rattles briskly across the pink and gold pavings using two flat-irons for propulsion. Inside, the atmosphere is equally relaxed. People do not feel constrained to talk in whispers. The vast carpeted expanse of the

Mosaic patterns in the Great mosque

uncluttered floor and the high decorated beams of the flat roof above absorb the small waves of human sound in an ocean of calm. The carpets of the nave – and to Christian eyes the prayer hall is all nave, 130 metres of it divided into three aisles, with no focal point, such as an altar, to break the perspective – are a vibrating harmony of reds: crimson, rose, Venetian red, burnt orange, softly blended. They make one glad one has no shoes. To tread on and on across that expanse of pile is in itself a soothing and unique experience. Overhead, every variety of chandelier blazes and glimmers in what seems an infinite recession of graceful shapes, picking out the edges of the tall Corinthian columns that run from end to end and touching the square-cut ceiling beams in the dusk overhead. There are odd, homely touches in this unfurnished hall of prayer. Against one pillar stands a forgotten grandfather clock, long stopped at twenty to eight. Near it, a huge wax candle – a grandfather candle – leans at an angle like a wonky chimney on a stand, once used to light the shrine of John the Baptist before electricity made the chandeliers blaze. On the carpets, Muslims kneel to pray where the fancy takes them, rocking on their haunches, telling their beads, or abasing themselves oblivious of the passers-by, the group visits, those who are seeking instruction from the turbanned mullahs, those stretched out propped on one elbow in an immemorial Arab posture, those who have gone to sleep. Without pews to get in the way, there is room enough for all to do as they like – even to take photographs. At the centre of the transept, under the dome, is a dais enclosed by wooden railings where old men in white skullcaps and brown gowns lean to talk amiably or meditate singly. Opposite this enclosure is the *mihrab*, or prayer niche, indicating the direction of Mecca, towards which the congregation

The wide spaces of the prayer hall

faces to pray. Beside it stands the pulpit. Women worshippers, heavily shrouded in black veils, sit in railed-off pens along the opposite wall, farthest from the prayer wall. The Muslims relegate women almost to the role of spectators at a distance – a strange difference from Christian practice, whose churches would be denuded of much more than half their congregations without the active participation of women. There is no

ordained priesthood in Islam. Every Muslim is as good as every other Muslim but some are more learned than others, having devoted their lives to study. Over by the prayer wall, an adult group, all male, is receiving instruction from a grey-bearded mullah in a white turban. They sit around him in a semi-circle, cross-legged and barefooted, like children in a primary school might in the West. The *ulemas* who instruct and preach are respected for their learning and the holiness of their lives, established by popular esteem. It is a very democratic system.

No one questions the right of a Christian to be present – though some mosques exclude them during the main prayer-hours on the Sabbath. There is complete tolerance in Islam for other religions. We have inherited from the Crusades the belief that Muslims and Christians necessarily regard each other as infidels, which was not the teaching of the Prophet. The Koran is full of the stories of Old Testament figures, Abraham, Noah, Moses and many more, and has sections devoted to John the Baptist, Jesus and his mother Mary. How else does one explain the shrine in the Great Mosque in honour of its most sacred relic, the head of John the Baptist? Its shining, bottle-green cupola dominates the long aisle and draws people to gaze through the grilles at the massive sarcophagus, covered with a cloth embroidered in Arabic script, which is believed to contain the Baptist's head, struck off by request of Salome. How the head came to be buried on this spot is difficult to account for, but tradition says it was and that is why the basilica of St John was erected here when Christianity became the official religion of the Byzantine empire. When Walid demolished the Christian church, he ordered a memorial column to be erected above the saint's tomb found in the crypt. This was succeeded by a wooden mausoleum which perished in the fire of 1893. The present shrine was then built in marble, richly decorated and gilded. Muslims venerate the Baptist under the Arab name of Yahya Ibn Zachariah – John the son of Zacharias – and you will see many of them at all times of day praying towards it and touching it as a holy shrine. There is another survival of the Christian church which has been preserved at the far end of the prayer hall – the Christian font. It is a large marble basin set beside an ancient well, which has been sealed. Both were used for infant baptism by total immersion fifteen centuries ago.

Though it is so large, there is about the Great Mosque a feeling of intimacy, serenity and freedom to commune with whatever spiritual power one believes in. It is easy and natural to fall into conversation in such a

Women dressed for mosque-going

place with people of another faith. One of the white-turbanned *ulemas*, his beard thrusting forth in two grey waves either side of his chin, settles comfortably back on his knees – a posture which takes long training to maintain – greets one encouragingly and gently expounds some basic tenets of Islam: mankind is one family, all men are brothers and all equal in the sight of God. There was true religion before Muhammad and before Jesus, who was a messenger sent from God to call the Jews back to true religion, which had become distorted to warlike ends since the days of Moses. Muslims, of course, regard Jesus as a normal human being, not

Ablutions in the mosque courtyard

as a divine one. So equally, was Muhammad, who received the most perfect revelation of God's will. The differences between Islam and Christianity are not, in Muslim eyes, fundamental. They have been exaggerated by money and politics. Both hold that it is not this life which is important but the life to come. In the calm sanctity of that atmosphere, it seems indeed that the divisions of faith might be easily healed.

Calm, however, is not a frequent attribute of Arab life. In the trading streets near the *suqs* you may find yourself dodging not only the traffic but a basin of water emptied out of an upper window. Syrians take sound and

colour in strong doses. Amid the ever-present cacophony of the tapes of Arab pop, on most street corners you will find a sweet shop assaulting the eye with glitter. Trays of crimson, gold, blue and purple wrapping on the bonbons are spread out in swathes of colours – no Arab shopkeeper would dream of shutting away such a gaudy sight in jars. The green-grocers hang up their wares in nets over their shopfronts making succulent swags of oranges, lemons and pomegranates. The leather shops are festooned with great bulging bags of hide or brightly dyed fur, interspersed with canvas gun cases, embossed saddles, pistol holders inlaid with

Washing the feet before prayer

bone, and serried cartridge belts, which suggest that the life of the old West and the life of the present East still have much in common. Even the dusky, gloomy windows often repay study. A window apparently full of brass flower-pots with handles turns out to be that of a fez-maker: the client is fitted for his fez by the simple method of trying them on him like upturned saucepans. And everywhere there is the glint of gold. In the goldsmiths' quarter adjoining the *suq* (open on Fridays because the goldsmiths are Christian, not Muslim) you may be surprised by the pendants and bracelets made entirely of British sovereigns and big £5 pieces of George V and Queen Elizabeth. They are not coins of the realm but copies, though warranted by the State as to their carat value and sold by weight. Syrians love all that glitters, even if it is not gold. They have a passion for coloured neon lights. Cafés flash their red and green and white lighted signs at you. And the long-distance buses, great dusty hulks by day, are strung with red, yellow, green and blue bulbs by night so that they come out of the dark twinkling like huge horizontal Christmas trees.

Obviously, in order to enjoy mixing and bargaining you have to be able to converse. A fair amount of English is spoken in the shops or, failing that, French, owing to the French occupation between the wars. But even a few words of Arabic open doors and make all the difference to the warmth of your reception. No visitor should shirk knowing at least enough to avoid appearing ignorant. A little time spent with a basic phrase book in the evening enhances the next day's casual encounters and also the chances of getting better service. Syrians are courteous people, almost ceremonious about greetings and thanks and goodbyes. The formulas for these go in pairs, like responses in church. This is not the place to teach vocabulary but at the least the visitor should

be ready with the most general word of greeting – *marhaba* – to which he will hear in response *marhabatayn* ('two greetings'), for the convention is that you must out-do each other in courtesy. The response to 'Good morning' – *sabah al-khair* – is *sabah an-nur*, which means literally 'morning of light'. But if it is after mid-day you must say 'Good evening' – *massah al-khair* – to which the answer is *massah an-nur*. Similarly, anyone who says 'thank you' – *shukran* – expects to be answered with *afwan* ('you are welcome'). *Naam* and *la* are 'yes' and 'no' and 'please' is *min fadlak*. People do not wish you health when drinking tea or coffee but two healths – *sahtayn* – and the right reply is *dayman*, which means 'always'. There are a multitude of flowery ways of saying goodbye but the most generally useful and easiest is *maa salema*, 'go with peace'. In any context, meeting or leaving, *salam aleikum* ('peace be with you') is irreproachable: the response is to put it the other way round, *aleikum salam*. You should also be familiar with two common interjections: *al-hamdu lillāh* ('praise be to Allah') and *insh'Allah* ('if Allah wills') which is applied to the making of any future plans.

Trading on the street is a Syrian custom and it seems that you can buy almost anything there – sweets and nuts, sherbet and cold drinks, hot cobs of sweet corn which people champ on as they walk along, littering the gutters with the stems like fat furry centipedes, combs and brushes, soap and scissors, knives and forks and kitchenware, scarves and shoes and dresses. The money-changers cluster with their suitcases near the entrance to the *suq*, ready to change any currency or traveller's cheque on a nearby windowsill. They offer a better rate of exchange than the hotels and a much quicker service than the banks, whose hours are short and whose queues are long. The principle Damascus works on is that anyone

The apprentice street trader

The artist and his model

who has anything to sell will do so wherever he happens to be. So you may come across an old bearded man holding up a fistful of ordinary tin-openers in hope. Another old man sitting on his doorstep in a fez may invite you into his front room to sell you something – perhaps a large bag of walnuts, which are excellent and remarkably cheap. On certain streets the bootblacks squat before their kerbside boxes of studded brass. The brass foot rest makes the centrepiece to the brass-railed trays on either side which hold rows of brass-lidded pots of polish. They will mix them, like artists from their palettes, to your exact shade. The whole transaction is a ceremony – brushing and washing clean, waxing, polishing, re-wax-

ing and re-polishing while the customer reads his newspaper or talks to his neighbour at the next stand. It is an artistic performance conducted at this shrine to the shoe and all for one Syrian pound!

In other streets you will find street photographers plying their trade between the parked cars with ancient tripod and black cloth. A photograph is still an event and soon attracts a crowd of fascinated onlookers. The photographers are ancient men, sporting a week's stubble, practising an ancient mystery. They do not operate either with a flash or in one. There is the positioning of the client against a black cloth hung over the railings; there is the squinting down a vertical eye-piece and the arrangement of the tripod. When all is set to their satisfaction, there is the ritual sweep with which the lens cap is removed, held for several seconds and replaced. The result, after mysterious fiddling in the interior of the camera wearing a black sleeve, is a negative. It is swished in a tray of hypo, washed in a battered tin of water, then propped up on a wooden slide projecting from the front of the lens to be photographed again. Five minutes later, with another flourish, the positive print is extracted from the entrails, washed, waved about to dry and offered for the admiration of the sitter and of the onlookers. It takes time, but what is time in Damascus when it is being devoted to an exercise in magic?

Considering their love of colour and display in other respects, Syrian dress is sadly unspectacular and subfusc. Those men who have not adopted western dress contrive to look drab and shapeless. The Syrian *galabiyah*, or full-length robe, is of fawn or dark brown or grey – unlike the Saudis' brilliant white – but its dignity is usually obscured by wearing over it a baggy western jacket of tweed or stripes, hanging well down the thigh. The *keffiyeh* head-dress of check is worn floppily over the top of that. It is held in place by the *ogal*, an encircling band of black hides, which when unwound forms a figure of eight and was originally designed as a halter for tethering the front legs of a camel. It is an elegant shape when hung in properly arranged folds, framing the ubiquitous black moustache and beard of the Syrian, but it does not go with the jacket. Some say the jacket is required for modesty but the reason for its popularity is more probably the pockets, which always seem to be bulging, thus adding still more to the rumpled, unpressed appearance of the wearer. Countrymen are still to be seen wearing pantaloons known as the *cheroual*. This unshapely garment hangs in a deep, low fold between the legs, having been designed in accordance with the tradition that the Prophet will one day be re-born of a man. Though it shows a pious readiness for this event, it does not add to the possibility of elegance.

Women, on the other hand, do not mix styles – they are either fully western or fully Arab in their dress. The older ones wear the black veil which shrouds the body and completely hides the face – they can see out through the fine mesh but you cannot see in. The majority, however, now wear western skirts and jumpers or dresses but adapt their beautiful scarves to serve as symbolic veils. Islamic convention holds that a woman's hair must not be seen by strangers so the scarves are very full and frame the face most attractively. One wonders how much longer this convention will last when one looks at the school-children, boys and girls dressed alike in a quasi-military uniform of greenish khaki drill, smart, disciplined and modern. Will they choose in later life to revert to the *galabiyah* or the veil? It seems unlikely. At the same time, much of the picturesqueness of the streets would be lost without traditional dress. The cafés opening on to the pavement are a portrait painter's dream. Cafés are for men only, as far as the Syrians are concerned. Bearded patriarchal figures in *galabiyah* and *keffiyeh* sit at the tables drinking glasses of sweet tea or Turkish coffee and drawing contentedly on the silver tube of a *narghilye* as they talk or play backgammon. Can one smoke a hubble-bubble in a two-piece suit? It seems that only the tourist would try. At night, under the blaze of harsh neon illumination, the clack of backgammon counters played at breakneck speed almost drowns conversation. No café is properly equipped without a stock of thirty or forty backgammon boards and bulbously gleaming silver hubble-bubbles which are brought to your

Turbanned *ulemas* carry their shoes across the mosque's marble courtyard

Aspects of devotion in the Omayyad Mosque

table with the drinks as a matter of course. A lighted coal of glowing tobacco is placed on top of the water container and by drawing on the mouthpiece the smoke comes cooled and filtered to the mouth. It is like smoking a pipe which never gets hot or too strong.

The swelling pomp of the Syrian belly is the natural end-product of Syrian food, which can be delicious but dauntingly copious to a European. The main meal of the day is lunch which begins with *mezza* – an hors d'oeuvre so lavish that you would take it for the main course – served to accompany the aperitif. Though the Prophet forbade the fermented juice of the grape, he said nothing about spirits, so it is a common sight for the first thing to appear at the table to be a bottle of whisky or arak, the clear, aniseed-tasting spirit which can be drunk like vodka, neat out of tiny glasses, or diluted with water. In the latter case it tastes like Greek ouzo, only stronger. But drunkenness is not a Syrian problem thanks to the amount and variety of dishes that accompany the drinks. *Mezza* may easily run to fifteen or twenty of them, purely as appetizers. There is humus, a mild version, made with sesame oil; a purée of aubergine with oil and lemon called *Baba Ghanouge*; a chopped salad of flat-headed parsley with onion and tomato (*Tabouleh*); various dishes made with boiled, crushed wheat (*Burgol*); aubergines stuffed with rice (*Yalanji*); meat rissoles encased in pastry (*Sambosik*); and a potent mixture of garlic (*Toum*), milk and olive oil. These are but a sample and they are subtle and delicious. All are eaten with flat, unleavened bread, like pita, which is torn into pieces to be dipped into them. Such a first course takes the best part of half-an-hour, interspersed with conversation, but it is usually followed by shish kebab wrapped in the warm folded bread or a charcoal-grilled half-chicken per person or *couscous*,

introduced by the French from Morocco. Syrians eat late into the afternoon, especially on Fridays when the cars wend their way in a column out of the city over the mountain road leading to the Lebanese border and Beirut. Open-air restaurants line the narrow green valley of the Barada river as it picks its poplar-lined way beneath the bare limestone heights to water the Damascene oasis which is called the *Ghouta*. As the road climbs around the bare, baked shoulders of Mount Kassioun, which sits golden and gleaming above the city, you can stop and look out over the vista of Damascus and out beyond it to the Golan Heights at the southern end of Mount Hermon. It is not difficult to understand why the Syrians feel menaced by the Golan Heights, the triple peak looming on the horizon. The southernmost summit of the three is in Israeli hands and all too clearly there are no natural obstacles between it and their capital, only forty miles away.

At Friday lunch at one of these open-air restaurants overlooking the Anti-Lebanon mountains, the *Jebel esh-Sharqi*, one may well wonder about the ambiguous position of women in modern Syria. There they sit, many of them as smartly westernized in dress and coiffure as any European woman, occupying the seat of power in the household and at the centre of the family lunch party (all Syrian family parties are large). The younger ones, married and unmarried, are often at the University of Damascus where women form a third of the student body and outnumber the men on many courses. They go to the over-crowded lectures in jeans and sweatshirts. They have never worn the veil and are never likely to. They take the pill. They smoke, though they seldom drink. They attend not only the arts courses but also medicine and engineering (very popular among women). They go into government offices and embassies and the headquarters of the big companies. They can, and do, join the army. There are six women members of the Syrian parliament and a woman minister – of culture. These days they go out for amusement to the plush-upholstered basement discos in the smart hotels, though social life more typically consists of visiting one another's houses most nights of the week. But they live in what is still very much a Muslim country which means that husbands are lords and masters of their wives. A man is still permitted four wives, as sanctioned in the Koran, but it is rare for him to be prepared or able to face the expense. It is also customary for a new wife to have to pass the test of approval by the first and senior wife. Such agreement is not easy to arrange. Divorce, though technically simple under Islamic law, is apparently not frequently resorted to. Women are far from being the chattels of men. They also take the lead in making decisions affecting the household. And yet, when it comes to their own lives, their independence is extremely limited. Girls are generally married very young, as young as fifteen in many cases. The prospective husband begins by seeking permission of the girl's parents; among the poorer classes her wishes may not even be consulted, though in educated families she has the right to refuse a man she does not love or want to marry. Virginity is vital and a bride who did not have it may well be sent back to her parents. In all this, Syrian women seem to concur. The earlier they are married, the luckier they think they are. And the men see early marriage as nothing but an advantage. 'The younger a girl is when she is married, the better,' said one. 'She will come to you for guidance as she did to her parents. She is made of such soft material that she can be moulded as you desire.'

One consequence of the sheltered upbringing of girls is that many Syrian men

Syrian beauty, unveiled

prefer to do the shopping for the household themselves. They reason that their wives have probably never known any men but their husbands and they do not want to give them the opportunity for casual encounters. And yet, now that women are free to take jobs and make careers of their own, surely this surveillance will be resented – and impractical? Well, it depends what you mean by free. In Syria, the freedom of women is relative. A pretty and intelligent young woman student, married and with children, said that on getting her degree at Damascus University, she would like to become a teacher, 'but, of course, it will

The coffee drinkers

A courtyard behind the *suq*

The *keffiyeh*, patterned in black and white

come home she must be there. The meal must be ready. To have a wife at home, waiting for you, is happiness. Paradise!'

The life of modern well-to-do Damascenes centres today on the lower slopes of Mount Kassioun. Embassies, apartment blocks and French-style restaurants with terraces line the leafy streets, like the European quarter of many Eastern Mediterranean cities. But the life-style of the old pashas and rich merchants can still be glimpsed in the Old City, where some of their houses survive. The showpiece of these is the Azem Palace, built in 1749 for the Ottoman governor of Damascus, Assad Pasha al-Azem, whose descendents continued to live here until 1920. It stands just south of the Great Mosque, whose minarets overlook its creeper-hung courtyards. These are surrounded with colonnades of Moorish arches in horizontally-striped stone. A pleasing domestic touch are the little domed lanterns with hanging tassles suspended from each arch. It is a peaceful oasis. Full grown trees of spruce and cypress and citruses laden with fruit (for marmalade) give shade to the rose beds and the expanses of black and pink marble paving-stones. A slow-trickling fountain soothes the ear. The palace is divided into two wings, the family wing set round its courtyard – the *haramlik* – and the guest wing – the *salamlik*. The courtyard of the harem – the ladies of the household had the most attractive part – is served by an old revolving wooden hatch through which food was passed from the kitchens so that no male guest could catch a glimpse of their cloistered beauty. The walls of the interior are of polychrome stone, decorated with mosaics and stalactites of carved and painted wood. They are almost oppressively ornate.

The Palace is now the Museum of the Arts and Popular Traditions of Syria and the rooms are used as settings for life-size dioramas of wax figures illustrating traditional

depend on what my husband wants. I couldn't take a job unless he wanted me to. It is up to him.' Her husband, sitting farther along the lunch table, did not pause for a moment when asked, 'Would you like your wife to become a teacher?' 'She will be a wife,' he announced definitively. Why? 'For my happiness.' The answer was self-evident to him. The other Arab men around the table agreed. 'Happiness is a wife at home,' said one, 'a man should not have to look after himself. A man should not have to cook.' Another chimed in; 'While I am at work, she can go out as much as she pleases – to visit her friends – but when I

Suq staircase, worn down over the centuries

Syrian scenes – a wedding ceremony or a pasha's reception. In the entrance hall can be seen a portrait of the unlucky and extravagant Azem Pasha himself – he ruled Damascus for fifteen years and was then hanged by his Turkish overlords. There is also a sepia photograph of the last pasha who handed over his house to the French when they occupied the city in 1920 – a fine, white-whiskered and bearded Edwardian figure in court dress with gold frogging, leaning lightly against a button-back chair in his courtyard. Looking at both of them one gets a glimpse of the lords of feudal Damascus as it was before the twentieth century caught up with it.

Everyone is taken to see the Azem Palace as a superb example of Damascene domestic architecture but another example exists, still in family occupation, at the eastern end of the Street Called Straight – known in Arabic as *Bab Sharqi* street after the gate in the city walls to which it leads. This street is the axis of the old city, the west to east artery that was much broader when St Paul knew it and recovered his sight there. It was then called the *Via Recta* and was the main thoroughfare of the Roman street pattern. It is a mile long and is intersected at right angles by side streets, dividing the old city into quarters, one of them Christian (on your left), another Jewish (on your right). Nowadays it is a babel of horns as buses, vans and three-wheelers struggle to squeeze past each other without knocking over the goods which are stacked on the pavements outside the shops. Two-thirds of the way along, going east, a ruined Roman arch sticks out into the street as a reminder of the old Roman main street, or Decumanus. At the extreme end, the third-century Roman East Gate, the *Bab Sharqi*, half original, half restored, still channels the traffic through the best-preserved section of the old city walls. Passing through it, into the bedlam

of lorries following the ring road round the line of the walls, you will find an ancient shop-front inscribed with the name of Georges Nassan – 'All Sorts of Antiquities'. This is the most renowned craft workshop in Damascus. Inside, passing the antique counter, you first find a spinning shop equipped with venerable wooden Jacquard looms. After that comes the cabinet-making shop where they prepare the wood and bone inlays for which Damascus is famous. They will show you how they bind and glue together long slivers of valuable rosewood, lemonwood, walnut, green pistachio and strips of camel bone which make the white ornamental inserts in the pattern. All these are pressed together in star-shaped bundles and then sliced into very, very thin cross-sections to make star-shaped pieces for the jigsaw puzzle of the veneer. The rosewood is cut from rose trees which must be seventy-five years old. This is the most expensive of the materials. The camel bone, though beautiful, is not. It comes from the city slaughterhouses, where camel meat is still sold for the market. Those who have tried it claim it is delicious – 'as good as mutton'. The inlaid boxes and tables and stools one sees here are tributes to the craftsmen's patience. Even an ordinary inlaid box contains over 500 pieces. To make a big cabinet takes six months. The inlay work is done by men, not women; damask cloth and embroidery are the women's province. The Kurds specialize in silk brocade. All these luxuries, together with brass, silver and gold work, are available from this family business of the Nassans, which began 180 years ago. The crates awaiting despatch to the United States and Europe bear witness to its worldwide clientele.

If you are lucky, you may also be shown the house which lies behind the workshops, a rich Damascene merchant's house which is still very much lived in, as well as being

A fez-maker with the tools of his trade

Romantic fiction on display

Old clothes for sale

in demand for government receptions and parties and as a setting for film and television companies.

The house, built 300 years ago, is centred round a courtyard, a combination of an outdoor living-room and garden. In the centre of it an octagonal pool and marble fountain is filled with pink Damask roses and a vine-trailing arch shades the paving. At one end of the courtyard is a typically Damascene invention, an *Iwan* – a raised and colonnaded dais roofed over for shade which looks out down the length of the courtyard. Its walls are picked out in cooling blue and green tiles and the mosaic floor is strewn with rugs and wide antique couches for the family and guests to relax on during hot summer evenings. Two old copper samovars stand in the corners. The house built round the rectangle of the courtyard is of two storeys, each for its own season. The ground-floor rooms are used in summer, because their two-foot-thick walls keep them cool; the upper floor is used in winter because it is warmed by the sun. This was the traditional Syrian pattern of living. The Nassan family, who bought the house in 1865, maintain another Syrian tradition: when the sons of the family grow up and marry, they are given apartments around the courtyard in which to raise their families. Arabs do not feel the necessity to leave the parental roof.

The present Mr Georges Nassan, now in his seventies with a lean, wise Syrian face, is the grandson of the family patriarch Giorgios Nassan, who bought the house and lived to the age of 115. It was in his time that the firm had the distinction of making the brocade for the Coronation robes of Queen Elizabeth of England, woven with silver and twenty-one carat gold thread and given to her as a present from the Syrian government. The brocade was the original of the 'love bird' design which is still made for their customers. He has lived in the house all his life. 'I like it – my wife doesn't,' he says. 'So many rooms mean having a lot of servants and upkeep. After all, the middle of the house is open to the sky and the rain. For ten years we moved out to a modern apartment on the slopes of Mount Kassioun. But in the end I came back. I was happier here.' When you examine the rooms grouped around the courtyard, you can well understand why. The house is virtually a living museum. The rooms have been decorated by three generations of the family to exhibit their craftsmen's work. Only millionaires could now afford to have such rooms reproduced to order – and some of them still do. One room is an oriental salon. Half of the floor space is raised and floored with wood for warmth in winter. The other half is marble, inset with a marble water basin, for coolness in summer – a sort of primitive air conditioning. Round the panelled walls is a range of sepia family portraits going back for 120 years. It is like being enclosed in a cabinet of photographs. The chairs, fifty years old, are made of walnut with intricate bone inlay and upholstered in silk brocade. Only four such sets of furniture have been made. A few years ago a Dane paid £10,000 to have the five-piece suite reproduced. Room succeeds room, almost stifling in the richness of their decoration which completely covers walls and ceilings. It is like living inside a series of richly carved wooden boxes. Some have stained-glass friezes. Some have cornices fringed with dangling glass beads. Long, low divan seats stretch all round the walls. Above them the wooden wall panels open to reveal cupboards, deeply recessed in the massive thickness of the mud walls. They were used for storing mattresses and bedding during the daytime, for clothes or for storing food, according to the function of the room. With every wall a closet, there

The line from Damascus to Beirut

The Suleimaniye Mosque, built by the Turks in 1554

is no problem in keeping a room uncluttered, except for cushions and benches to
loll on. One room is called 'The Thousand
and One Nights' and one can imagine no
more appropriate setting for Scheherazade,
telling her tales to an audience seated on the
floor or the divans and leaning back against
the cushions. On certain nights the family
give their own parties in Arab costume with
Arab dancers and hubble-bubbles to enter-

tain the guests. Such was the way of life of
old Damascus. Now only a handful of such
homes survive and are lived in. The craftsmen who make such marvels of Arab art-
istry are dying out and their skills are not
being passed on. 'This sort of work will last
for another thirty, perhaps fifty years,' said
Mr Nassan with resignation.

The same can, sadly, be said of so much
that constitutes the present charm of Damas-

cus. The fez can now only be seen on the heads of the older generation. Gradually the fine old men in skullcaps and *galabiyah*, who seem to have an eternity in which to talk to one another, will pass away, as have so many of the chaotic but venerable buildings. What is taking their place is the same all over the world. Concrete high-rise building, traffic choking on itself, the anonymous crowd of suits and skirts – all these are designed for a hurried, crowded, standardized age. At least in Damascus, the process has not gone far enough to rub out variety and individuality. The Old City is safe from 'improvement'. The mosques dream serenely on and the *suqs* bustle with frenzy under their high, black roofs, still giving the traveller a sense of time's continuity; strutted balconies still totter precariously over the trickling Barada; more balconies overhang

Closed for siesta

the little lanes which wander crookedly off the Street Called Straight; horses pull carts through the narrowest of alley-ways and donkeys plod under their bulging loads among the passers-by. Life is always ready to stop for another glass of hot, sweet, black tea or a leisurely hour over the hubble-bubble. The wavering cadences of the *muezzin* still call out across the rooftops – especially at 4 a.m. when the city is stilled and the traffic cannot drown the haunting music of the Koran as it has sounded for thirteen centuries over these streets. Damascus is a chaos of conflicting centuries. But at least it is a chaos unmistakably its own, like no other capital in the world.

SYRIA
BEFORE CHRIST

THE 'FERTILE Crescent' stretches through the Near East in a sickle-shaped arc from the apex of the Persian Gulf, up the plain between the rivers Tigris and Euphrates, around the foot-hills of Northern Syria below the Taurus Mountains, and sweeps down parallel with the Mediterranean coast into Palestine. If you imagine that the sickle blade has a handle, it would project up the valley of the Nile to Upper Egypt. It is along this Fertile Crescent that civilized man made his earliest agricultural settlements and Syria lies along the central section of the blade. Western Syria is dotted with ancient sites. So is the valley of the Euphrates on its north-eastern borders. This was the most important section of the world for the first three thousand years of man's recorded history. Indeed, it *was* the world. When Europeans first aspired to civilized and settled life, it had already been proceeding along the Fertile Crescent for over 2000 years. The first agriculture, the first cities, the first empires, the first written languages, the first alphabets were all founded along its length. So were the first two monotheistic religions, Judaism and Christianity, and later it became the adopted centre of the third, Islam.

In a land of such antiquity and historical influence as Syria it is necessary to know something of the sweep of history, especially ancient history, to appreciate the relics that lie all about you. This is no easy matter. Not only is the history of Syria, as part of the Ancient World, immensely long and complicated, it is being rewritten every year as new archaeolological discoveries come to light. Our knowledge of most of the 3000 years before Christ consists of small islands of dusky light in an ocean of obscurity. It is a detective quest which has only reached its early stages. So much remains to be discovered – and so much will never be discovered – that for most of those three millennia before Christ, let alone before that, we are in the realm of opinion and interpretation, not fact. For example, it has long been assumed that Syria was the buffer zone, and often the battle-ground, between the kingdoms at the two opposite ends of the Fertile Crescent – those of ancient Egypt, with its pharoahs and pyramids to the west, and of Mesopotamia, with its succession of city-states, Sumer, Akkad and Babylon, to the east. Certainly Syria was frequently invaded and ruled from both East and West. But recent – some extremely recent – discoveries have shown that Syria itself produced cities that held empire over large areas of this land, the city-kingdoms of Mari, Ebla, and Ugarit. Their sites have been exposed, their treasures found, their tablets deciphered. The result is that anyone who visits Syria in ignorance of the misty history of these once-mighty civilizations is missing much of the excitement and fascination of the country, perhaps almost half the point of coming. There are few museums in the world of as much interest and importance for the period before Greece and Rome (and as blessedly calm and uncrowded) as those of Damascus and Aleppo.

It is very hard, without prolonged study,

to visualize the overall sequence of events in the three millennia before Christ. What follows is necessarily an over-simplified sketch of the outstanding eras of early Syrian history.

Who were the people who lived here? They were migrants who came northwards from Arabia, in quest of new land and resources. They found not only land but the possibility of domestic agriculture, settled and changed their nomadic way of life. There seem to have been peaks of migration at intervals of roughly every thousand years. Mesopotamia was colonized about 3500 BC by nomad tribes who became the Sumerians, Akkadians and Babylonians. Syria, and its adjoining territories to the west and south, was settled about 2500 BC by the incoming Amorites and Canaanites. The Amorites settled in the interior and the Canaanites in the coastal land, later becoming known as the Phoenicians. About 1500 BC the Arameans and the Hebrews began to spread into these lands. In 500 BC the Nabateans appeared. And soon after AD 600 the Muslim Arabs advanced from Mecca to establish the Islamic empire. All these people are known as Semites – 'Semite' means descended from Shem, the son of Noah. All of them spoke closely related languages known as Semitic – Akkadian, Canaanite, Aramaic, Hebrew and Arabic were all evolved from similar roots and have many resemblances, finally resulting in the common tongue of Arabic. Syria was a melting pot of Semitic peoples and civilizations, sometimes invaded from Egypt, sometimes from Babylon, sometimes from the mountains to the north by the Hittites. Then came the Persians under Darius, the Greek armies of Alexander the Great and the Roman legions led by Pompey and his successors. During this period of conquest and change, three Syrian native empires rose and fell. The first was at Mari, which stands

near the banks of the Euphrates at the extreme south-east corner of modern Syria, near the border with Iraq. It is now called Tell Hariri. The surface of Syria is dotted with Tells, or mounds, built up from the surrounding land like sugar loaves. They are the burial mounds of ancient towns, whose mud walls and dwellings crumbled and fell down. The next inhabitants simply levelled the ruins and built on top of them. Sooner or later the town was abandoned and the wind and sand did the rest, covering the layers up for centuries, often for millennia, sometimes for ever. Nobody knows what lies under dozens of unexplored Tells in Syria. But in 1933, at Tell Hariri, a Bedouin searching for a stone to mark a grave disinterred one from the ground and found it was a headless statue, subsequently identified as the sun god Shamash. The archaeologists got busy excitedly. By now we know they were standing on top of not just a settlement but of a capital city – Mari, capital of the Kingdom of Amurru or Hani, which flourished from about 2700 BC to 1750 BC. They found the palace of the last king, Zimiri-Lim, and could not believe its size. It had 300 rooms, some of whose mural paintings still survived; there were bathrooms with ceramic baths; there was an archive of between 20,000 and 30,000 tablets written in cuneiform script in the Akkadian language; they found temples and statues of the kings of Mari and their goddesses, especially of Ishtar, the goddess of fertility and of war. And beneath the palace of King Zimiri-Lim they found the foundations of another palace dating back a thousand years earlier to 2700 – the era when the Great Pyramids and the Sphinx were being erected by Cheops and the pharoahs of the Fourth Dynasty of Egypt. By the time that Zimiri-Lim was King of Mari he ruled over much of Mesopotamia. The city of Akkad under its great king, Sargon, had risen and fallen

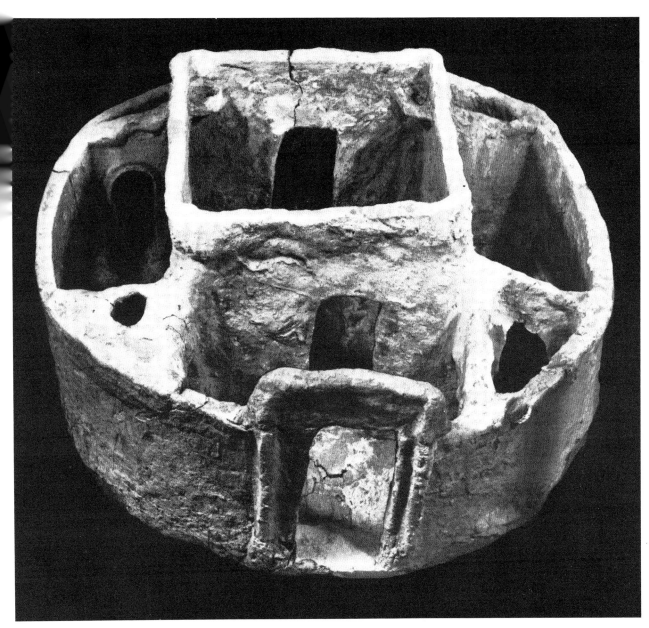

Clay models of a round house.
Mari (Tell Hariri). *Photo: Horst Klengel*

Alabaster statue of Ibu-Shamagan, from Mari.
Photo: Horst Klengel

. . . and left no trace to this day of where it stood. To the east the new power was Babylon and it was Hammurabi of Babylon, author of the first code of laws, who defeated Zimiri-Lim and destroyed Mari for ever.

It is possible, though arduous, to visit the Mari excavations and marvel at the mud brick walls and courtyards of what was a complex and sophisticated city that thrived when, in Ancient Britain, men had probably not begun to build Stonehenge. But the treasures are nearly all in the museums of Damascus and Aleppo and that is where to appreciate them. The statues are large by the standards of their epoch and made of alabaster. The kings and priests of the city stare at us with huge, doll-like eyes, their heads shaven, their hands clasped in adoration of their gods. They wear nothing but curious ritualized long skirts, called *Kaunakes*, that at first sight remind one of plumage or even the ruffles round a wedding cake. Perhaps the most striking statue of all this epoch is the stately goddess holding a vase from which the water flowed into the fountain of the Great Palace. She is to be found in the Aleppo Museum. Her counterpart in the National Museum at Damascus is a temple singer and dancer called Ur-Nina. She sits cross-legged and naked from the waist up with her long hair swept back severely from a centre-parting, looking at you with enormous blue eyes made of lapis lazuli. No one meeting her eyes and the almost cynical curl of her lips could doubt that here was a worldly and sophisticated woman of a highly developed culture. In Damascus Museum, too, you can see the 'treasure of Ur' – a collection of precious gifts sent to the king of Mari by the king of Ur, the great city of the Chaldees near the mouth of the Euphrates. It was found in a jar buried in the palace courtyard and it includes a bronze goddess, an ivory goddess

and a lion-headed eagle, whose wings of lapis lazuli contrast with its head and tail covered in gold leaf. These were the finest pieces of craftsmanship of their time. But the most human exhibit is an architect's clay model of a house dating back to the first period of Mari's pre-eminence, about 2500 BC. It is a circle built round an inner square, giving a most pleasing design of nine curved rooms opening through doorways onto a central courtyard. To look at it is to imagine what life in that house was like. It had privacy and it had style and a sort of organic beauty at a time when most of the human race was living in caves or mud huts.

The excitement of the discovery of Mari was repeated recently in 1968. A shepherd found a large trough or cistern made of basalt near a large and prominent Tell, Tell Mardikh, thirty-five miles south-west of Aleppo. It was carved in relief showing warriors, lions and a horned god with a sphinx. It is now in the Aleppo Museum and it looks like an old stone sink – but it was enough to start an Italian archaeologist, Dr Paolo Matthiae of Rome University, digging. The Tell was excavated for four seasons before a headless statue was unearthed with an Akkadian inscription in cuneiform script which declared that the statue was dedicated to the goddess Ishtar by Ibbit-Lim, 'king of the people of Ebla'. They had discovered the site of Ebla, a kingdom contemporary with Mari. Six more years of excavations exposed the foundations of a mud-brick palace and, in 1974, they found a library of forty-two clay tablets written in an unfamiliar language, since deciphered and named Eblaite. In the following year another, much larger, library was unearthed. The number of tablets has now reached 17,000, identifying Ebla beyond doubt. They are enabling us, as they are translated, to form a picture of its golden age which occurred from 2400 BC, when it ruled an empire, until 2250, when it was destroyed by fire and conquest by the Akkadian King, Naram-Sin.

Visiting Ebla is a curious experience. At first you cannot believe there is anything there. The dusty road to Tell Mardikh rises between acres of bare, scraped limestone ridges, through a beehive village, and winds up to the rounded plateau of the Tell, 140 acres of desolate, heaped earth in the middle of nowhere – far from the sea, far from the mountains, quite far even from the nearest signs of fertility in the Orontes valley. Why did men build a city here that supported a quarter of a million people? One can only suppose that in 4500 years the climate and vegetation have changed considerably. There must have been trees near here, big trees, for in the excavated audience hall of the palace there are circular sockets as big as wells, where stood the wooden pillars supporting the roof. The city was famous for its craftsmanship in wood, its furniture and carving. The throne of the King of Mari, carved out of precious wood, was made in Ebla. The receipt for it is duly noted in the tablets. Near the hollowed-out audience chamber workmen are pickaxing away crumbled mud in clouds of dust to reveal other structures. Looking down into the library – quite a small chamber – you can make out the sockets of the lines of shelves where the thousands of tablets were found, still stacked on edge like files in a filing cabinet, a tribute to the orderly minds of librarians of 4000 years ago. You can still see the black marks of the fire that destroyed the shelves they stood on in 2250 BC. The fire destroyed the palace but preserved the tablets by baking them even harder.

Perhaps the most eerie experience to be had in Ebla today is to stand on the slopes of the central Akropolis as the sun is going down across the empty plains beyond the city walls which encircle the Tell. The inhabitants of Ebla must have looked out from their city kingdom at exactly the same sunset over the same landscape. Everything else in their world has vanished but the view at sunset remains the same. Professor Matthiae, bronzed by the sun, works here from August to October every year assisted by his university students. Was he surprised when the site he was working on turned out to be Ebla? No, he told me, he knew the Tell was the right size and of the right era. The tablets were the real surprise – they were the most sensational discovery of archaeology in recent years. The world is still waiting to learn what they contain in detail. The work of translation, by Dr Giovanni Pettinato, is an immense task of scholarship. We are dealing here with one of the earliest written languages in the world, older even than Akkadian, in the opinion of Professor Matthiae. Eblaite was a mature, developed language before the Akkadian language appeared and so it can claim to be the origin of the Semitic languages such as Babylonian, Phoenician and Aramaic and, therefore, the original source of both modern-day Hebrew and Arabic.

The significance of Ebla was underlined to me by Dr Kassem Toueir, of the National Museum of Damascus: 'This discovery has changed all the facts about the early history of the Near East. The Ebla state archives have provided us with the first documents on this era written from a Syrian point of view. We are now sure that Syria was not a secondary arena of conflict between the big powers of Mesopotamia and Egypt. It was the third big power. It controlled an immense territory from Mesopotamia to the coast. It had good commercial relations with Egypt. It even, astonishingly, had relations with the far-away King of Khamazi, in Eastern Persia. We have discovered in the tablets the first diplomatic letter, written from King Irkub-Damu of Ebla to King Zizi of Khamazi, in which he calls him "My brother" and

Statue of a goddess of water, about 1800 BC Mari. *Photo: Horst Klengel*

asks him to send him some good soldiers in return for a gift of gold brocade clothing and precious furniture. Other tablets in the archive record treaties between the kings of Ebla and Sargon I, King of Akkad, and the first King of Assur, Tutiya, the founder of the Assyrian dynasty. Another, perhaps the earliest known military despatch, gives the news that the city of Mari has been defeated. The King of Ebla, in about 2400 BC, ruled over Mari and appointed his brother as its king.'

But, above all, we know now that Eblaite was the earliest Semitic language. And all this knowledge has only been discovered in the past three or four years. No wonder that Naram-Sin, the King of Akkad, boasted on a monument of his victory over so great a kingdom: 'I, Naram-Sin, king of the four directions, conqueror of Ebla and Armanum which had never been destroyed before me since the creation of the world.'

It was not the end of Ebla. Life returned to the ruins about 1900 BC and the city prospered again for 300 years before being destroyed by the Hittites. King Ibbit-Lim, whose headless statue first identified the site of Tell Mardikh as Ebla, was the last of its kings. After his city fell there was nothing on the site except a small village in Graeco-Roman days. Ebla disappeared from history. It left behind a puzzle: among the cities mentioned in the Ebla tablets, along with Damascus, Byblos and Gaza, are the Biblical cities of Sodom and Gomorrah, and among the Canaanite personal names are such easily recognizable Biblical names as Ab-ra-mu, E-sa-um and Da-u-dum. This gave rise to excited but ill-informed controversy about the possibility that they indeed referred to the Biblical figures of Abraham, Esau and David. Dr Matthiae and others dismiss this as nonsense. Ebla flourished at least a thousand years before the patriarchs of the Old Testament. All that the tablets prove is that

such names as Abraham were common long before those events. The god El was worshipped at Ebla – El simply means 'God' – but there is no mention of Yahweh or Jehovah.

So Ebla fell for the second time, along with Mari, around 1600 BC and the stage was cleared for the next important Syrian kingdom, the city of Ugarit which rose to greatness beside the sea, five miles north of Latakia at a place now called Ras Shamrah. Ugarit was discovered as long ago as 1928 – again by the chance discovery of a peasant who ploughed up a vault containing pottery. It is a much larger site than Ebla and more impressive to visit because its ruins are of stone. The first thing you see is the gate into the fortress, shaped like an inverted V sloping backwards in line with the stone defence walls. Ugarit used to stand beside the sea. The shore line has now retreated from it by 300 feet. Outside this gate, where the local boys now play football, stood its busy harbour, trading with Egypt and Mycenae and Cyprus, whose north-eastern tip lies opposite it across the sea. In time of attack, the population of the harbour could withdraw through this V-shaped gateway and up the zig-zagging flight of stone steps into the royal palace forecourt. When you climb the mound, you reach the paved palace courtyard, still provided with a fountain, circular pedestals for sentries and the palace gateway with slots cut in the stone to take the great wooden gates. Beyond lies the shallow stone fish-pond and the deep vaults of the royal cemetery. The kings of Ugarit were buried upright in pottery urns, supplied with food and gold for the after-life. On exposure to the air the urns crumbled to dust. The palace, one of the biggest of its time, had ninety rooms and an elaborate system of wells and cisterns and stone water channels. Under Ugarit's civilized law, minor offenders were sentenced to draw 100 buckets of water from the well to fill the cistern. Behind the palace lies the residential quarter of the town, acres of houses and winding alley-ways snapped off at waist or shoulder height. You need a guide to make sense of this fascinating jumble. The houses are still supplied with three essentials – a well, drainage and an underground family tomb. One of these is amazingly well preserved, the stone perfectly dressed and untouched by time. A flight of steps leads down into the vaulted crypt, where the potted remains of parents and grandparents were stored in their burial jars, while you continued to live on the floors above until it was your turn. It must have been a disconcerting thought. When the family crypt was full up with ancestors, you had to get permission to empty the oldest burial jar – all deaths were registered – and the bones it contained were dropped into a bone pit which can still be seen through an opening in the floor. The bones were found – the jars perished. In one house were found the skeletons of a family who perished in the invasion which destroyed Ugarit towards 1200 BC. They were those of a man, a woman and a young girl. The girl was still wearing her gold necklace and the man's skeletal hand was still clutching his dagger. In another section you can see the stables and the wells used for watering the horses. The narrow streets twist their way between the cut-off walls, sprouting scrub and thorn bushes. It is not hard to imagine them alive again with Canaanites as they were on the day when it was destroyed by the northern invaders known as 'the People from the Sea'.

But the greatest find at Ugarit was the alphabet – the most ancient alphabet yet known – dated from about 1400 BC. What a breakthrough this was for the human race! Until then there had been two kinds of writing – Egyptian hieroglyphic and Mesopotamian cuneiform, both requiring hundreds

of signs and far too difficult for any but the scribes to use. The Ugaritic scribes also used a cuneiform reed pen, or stele, to make arrow-head-shaped impressions in moist clay but they had the brilliant inspiration to make thirty letters to represent consonantal sounds which could be used again and again. Simple, it seems now – incredible it must have seemed then: the whole key to writing, the thirty signs, could be inscribed on a little piece of clay the size of a finger. This is how it was found and a scale model of it can be bought at the site or at the National Museum at Damascus, where the original finger of clay is one of the prize exhibits behind three layers of security glass. It looks like a diagram of Semaphore signs. But consider what it did for the world. It was taken over the sea by the Phoenicians, who developed it by adding curves to the signs, and it was adapted and adopted by the Greeks and the Romans, to give Europe its ABC – or rather ABC, which is the order the Greeks use still. Many tablets were written in this alphabet in Ugaritic, which shares some 700 words in common with modern Arabic. Besides the palace archives, two religious libraries and two private libraries were discovered and among them were tablets of mythological poems, some of the oldest in civilization, six hundred years older than the *Iliad* and the *Odyssey*. There were also tables of weights and measures and dictionaries for translating Ugaritic into Babylonian or Akkadian, the international language of the time. The treasures of Ugarit show what a rich city it was and also what leaps forward in craftsmanship there had been since the time of Mari and Ebla. At the Damascus National Museum you will find the miraculous little gold statuette of the god Baal, the supreme god of the Canaanites who lived at Ugarit, to whom they built their greatest temple. There is also a striking miniature ivory head of Baal which is one of the most

An ivory head. One of the most beautiful single finds from Ugarit. *Photo: Horst Klengel*

beautiful of pre-Greek sculptures. Though it has lost its gold leaf coating and the coloured stones that were inlaid for the eyes, it is perhaps even more attractive in the austerity of ivory.

What happened in Syria after the fall of Ugarit until the arrival of Alexander the Great is complex. The Arameans arrived from the South and merged with the Canaanites and Amorites, introducing their language, Aramaic, which gradually established itself as the vernacular throughout Syria and, indeed, the whole Near East. Syria fell to the Assyrians, under Tiglath-Pileser III, who captured the Aramean kingdom of Damascus in 732 BC. The Assyrians in turn were displaced by the new Babylonian empire of Nebuchadnezzar, who had conquered all Syria and Palestine by 572 and who deported the tribes of Israel. In 538 mighty Babylon itself fell to the Persians under Cyrus the Great. Syria became a province of the Persian empire which, for 200 years, stretched from Egypt to the borders of India. This was the end of the Semitic empires of antiquity, for the Persians were Indo-European by race. So were the conquerors who followed them: Alexander the Great and his Macedonians in 333, who conquered Syria on his triumphal marches to Egypt and Persia and planted the land with Greek colonies and cities. His empire fell to pieces on his death in Babylon in 323. Syria fell to one of his four competing generals, Seleucus, who founded the Seleucid empire – and calendar – in 312. He founded thirty cities on the Hellenic street pattern, which included his capital Antioch (named after his father), Apamea, his military base (named after his wife) and Laodicea (named after his mother) which is now Latakia. Nothing of this period remains except the lonely but magnificent ruins of Apamea, which are described in the chapter on Aleppo. The Seleucid empire also fell apart

and in 169 the Nabateans began to dominate Southern Syria with their kingdom based on Petra (now in Jordan) and their Syrian chief city, Bosra. The Nabateans were Arabs, speaking Arabic, writing Aramaic, borrowing their architecture from the Greeks, successful traders and fine potters and craftsmen. Their own distinctive script formed the basis for written Arabic. A Nabatean king was invited by Damascus to be its ruler in 85 BC and protect it against the endless wars between the small states into which Syria had split up. He even drove back Pompey when the Roman forces first appeared in Syria. When, in 64 BC, Pompey made all Syria into a Roman province, the Nabatean king paid a lump sum in tribute and was allowed to keep Damascus. Rome's grip on Syria was for a long time insecure. The Romans were at war with the Parthians who drove them out of nearly the whole of the territory. Julius Caesar paid a visit and Mark Antony was briefly and ineffectively in command from 40 to 36 BC. Finally the anarchy abated under Augustus, the first emperor, and Syria was ruled as a Roman protectorate with local autonomy, retaining its own languages of Aramaic and Greek, its religions and its customs. The Roman governor of Syria, with his four legions, ranked equal in importance with the governor of Gaul. Syria was still a polyglot society of Arameans, Arabs, Jews, Phoenicians and Greeks, mingled in their own communities with their own local rulers, like Palmyra and its kings. A chain of Roman military posts stretched along the desert frontier with Parthia. Nomadic life was more or less over. Settled prosperity began. But Syria was still a Semitic country and about to play host both to Christianity and then to Islam, as the next chapter will tell.

A gold bowl from Ugarit, found near the temple of Baal. *Photo: Horst Klengel*

The basin carved with lion's heads and warriors whose discovery at Tell Mardikh started the excavations which uncovered Ebla

Under the bare mound of Tell Mardikh, near Aleppo, was discovered the city of Ebla, and the biggest archaeological discovery of recent years – a library of 17,000 clay tablets dating from the third millennium before Christ

Clay tablet from Ugarit. Thirteenth century BC

Painting from the great palace at
Mari of King Zimrilim,
c.1800 BC. The picture shows a
section of a sacrificial procession.
The hand covering part of the
head belongs to a much larger
figure leading the procession,
probably the king or priest

Alabaster statue of a woman named
Ur-Nina from Mari

Opposite: The Patriarch of Antioch, spiritual head of Syrian Christians

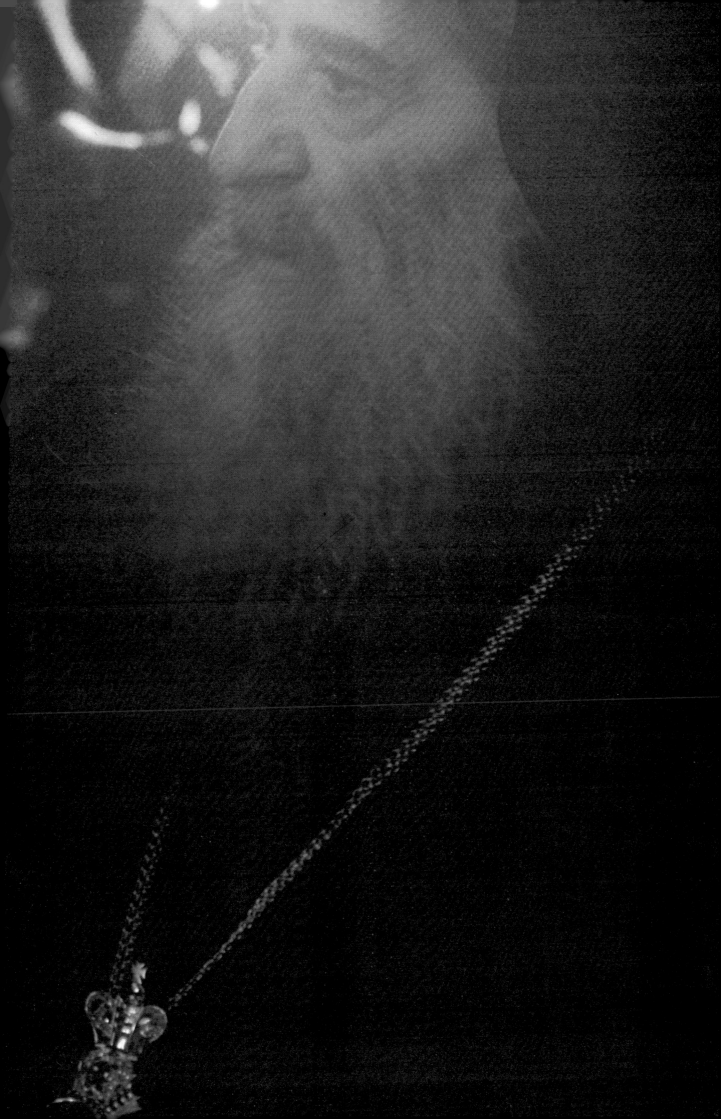

The Patriarch conducts a wedding at Saydanaya

Baptism by total immersion under the gaze of the ikons

CHRISTIANS AND MUSLIMS

DAMASCUS, LIKE Jerusalem, is one of the holy places both of the Christian and Muslim religions. It had a Christian community within a year or two of the Crucifixion and it was on his way to persecute this community that Saul of Tarsus underwent the extraordinary experience that converted him from an enemy to a saint called Paul. 'The Road To Damascus' has been synonymous with dramatic conversions ever since but it takes an effort of the imagination to grasp the magnitude of this event when it happened. Saul was a young Jewish student rabbi of the strictest sect, the Pharisees. He had been present at the stoning to death of Stephen, the first Christian martyr. He had even guarded the clothes of those who stoned him. There is no better account of the zeal with which he had tried to stamp out the new religion in Jerusalem than his own, as he gave it before King Agrippa: 'Many I shut up in prison, having received authority from the chief priests. And when they were put to death I gave my voice against them. And I punished them oft in every synagogue and compelled them to blaspheme. And being exceedingly mad against them I persecuted them even unto strange cities, whereupon I went to Damascus with authority and commission from the chief of priests. At midday, O King, I saw in the way a light from heaven, above the brightness of the sun, shining round about me and them which journeyed with me. And when we were all fallen to the earth, I heard a voice speaking in the Hebrew tongue, Saul, Saul, why persecutest thou me?'

Modern scholars date his conversion from as early as AD 31, about two years after they date the Resurrection and Pentecost. The place where he asked 'Who art thou, Lord?' and received the answer, 'I am Jesus, whom thou persecutest,' is said to be a hill called Kaukab, about six miles south of Damascus on the Jerusalem road, where there is now a modern shrine.

'And when I could not see for the glory of that light, being led by the hand of them that were with me, I came into Damascus,' said Paul nearly thirty years later in an impassioned speech to the crowd in Jerusalem which nearly lynched him. 'And one Ananias, a devout man came unto me and stood and said, Brother Saul, receive thy sight . . . the God of our fathers hath chosen thee.'

According to St Luke, who wrote these accounts in the Acts of the Apostles, Ananias, a devout Christianized Jew, was told in a vision to look for Saul of Tarsus in the house of Judas in the Street Called Straight. No one can now identify the house of Judas but the house of Ananias is carefully preserved by the Franciscans, who have built a modern church alongside it. It lies down a lane to the left of the Street Called Straight just before it reaches the eastern gate, the *Bab Sharqi*. It is a little, vaulted, underground crypt or chapel which no one could call beautiful. But it has survived the accidents of time while almost every other vestige of Roman (and early Christian) Damascus has been swept away. It was not underground in Paul's time. The twenty-three rocky steps leading to it take you down to the original level of the Roman street. Nearly 2000 years of rebuilding of the old city have raised its level by about fifteen feet. Down below, the bare stones are dimly lighted by two grilles cut in the vaulted roof. One of the two rooms is a chapel, decorated rather crudely with ikons. Sometime after the first century, Ananias's house was converted into a church, the Church of the Holy Cross. After the Muslim take-over it was converted into a mosque. Christians revered him as St Ananias, later first bishop of Damascus, and Muslims also revered him as Ananiyah. In the sixteenth century the Franciscan fathers wrote that both Christians and Muslims gathered in this little chapel to pray. So the little crypt, for all its ups and downs, and restorations, has a direct link with the New Testament and one of the longest histories of any church still extant. The same cannot be said of the *Bab Kaysan*, the tower gateway a little farther round the city walls to the south which is called 'St Paul's Window'. After receiving his sight, Paul stayed on in Damascus with the Christians he had come to arrest. He immediately began preaching in the synagogues that Jesus was the Son of God – to the amazement of the Jews. What a shock it must have been in that perplexed time that a strict Jew like Paul had been should suddenly have turned right round and claimed that the long awaited Messiah had already come and had risen from the dead. To those who believed it, his vision on the road to Damascus must have been accounted another miraculous appearance of Jesus after death – the last, indeed, of the series reported by the Apostles during the previous two years or so. It was hot news. We do not know how long it was before the traditional Jews made plans to kill this man whom they regarded as a traitor to their faith but St Luke tells us in the Acts that 'they watched the gates for him day and night'. It was then that the other disciples

'took him by night and let him down by the wall in a basket'. One would hardly have expected them to pick a spot where there was a gate. In any case this gate is far later than Roman times. It is Turkish in style. But Damascus has a legend that the gate which originally stood here was guarded by an Ethiopian Christian called Giorgios, who allowed Paul to escape by night and suffered execution for it. Paul himself says, in his Epistle to the Galatians, that after his revelation he went 'into Arabia and returned again to Damascus'. Three years later he went up to Jerusalem to see Peter and James, the brother of Jesus, and then went into the regions of Syria and Cilicia. What he meant by 'Arabia' is uncertain. As he did not go to Jerusalem then, it is unlikely he meant modern Arabia as this would have meant passing through Palestine. It seems more likely that he went into the Syrian desert to meditate on this complete reversal of all his previous beliefs before he began his arduous missionary journeys round the Eastern Mediterranean. The 'regions of Syria' in those days included far more than the country's present boundaries. 'Syria' has been used throughout history to mean a vaguely-defined area between Turkey in the north and the Sinai in the south. So it is probable that Paul stayed in Syria through those first years of his Christian conversion.

Syria had its share of saints in the early years of Christianity. One of the earliest was St Thekla, who was herself converted by Paul. She was the daughter of a governor in Asia Minor and, having heard Paul preach, left home and followed him, possibly to Damascus. After a time she settled down for life in a cave high up in the limestone ridge that runs fifty kilometres north of Damascus. A hill village called Maloula grew literally out of the rocks beneath her cave. Maloula is one of the sights of Syria. The narrow road from Damascus runs beside

Maloula clings crazily to its cliff-face

baked ochre hillsides, smoothed by time except for the limestone outcrop which marches along the top of them like a city wall built by giants, 4500 feet above sea level. Then comes a break in the parapet, a broken gorge through the line of hills, and a small oasis of fig trees, olives and poplars whispering in the breeze. The houses, little rectangular cells whose frontages are painted charmingly in powder blue and violet, are clustered along ledges backing into the cliff itself. They climb up and up until there are some which are no more than natural caves in the rock face plastered over with a front

The houses of Maloula grow haphazardly out of the caves in the cliff-face wall. Higher still are cell-like recesses in the rock, carved by nature, which are too high to be accessible. On the highest ledge to the left sits the Roman Catholic church of St Sergius (Mar Sarkis) with a small monastery attached to it. On the right, almost as high, sits the Orthodox convent of St Thekla, from which rocky steps lead up higher to her grotto – Mar Takla. The nuns conduct visitors to the grotto with its dripping roof. The water from the spring buried in the hillside is believed to have healing powers and many local people come to drink it. The cave, where St Thekla lived and is buried, is a shrine illustrated by ikons which depict the miracle-working powers attributed to her – you see her charming snakes and lions and standing unharmed in the midst of fire. No one knows quite why she chose to spend her life in this cave. Perhaps she was a natural hermit. Perhaps, as the nuns suggest, she preached in Damascus and, like Paul, had to flee and hide.

Maloula is not only one of the sights, but one of the sounds of Syria. The people who live there still speak Aramaic, or Syriac as it is also called, which was the language spoken by the whole of Syria and Palestine in the time of Jesus. Arabic, which gradually drove it out in Islamic times, is itself a development of Aramaic. By a quirk of history there are just three places left, Maloula and two nearby villages, where the inhabitants have hung on doggedly to their ancestral language. The children are still taught Aramaic as their first language to keep the tongue alive. But they cannot write in it – that knowledge has been lost except to specialist scholars. The differences are quite marked: Damascus – *Dimashq* in Arabic – is pronounced *Themseq* in Aramaic. Like many other townships in the region, Maloula is part Christian, part Muslim. The Christians have a priest and a town council, the Muslims a sheikh and their mosque. They live harmoniously side by side, united by their unique language and by pride in their cool and picturesque little town stuck to the cliff-side above its walled gardens in this small oasis of fertility.

Perhaps the most extraordinary of Syria's early Christians was St Simeon, also known as St Simon Stylites, who became famous throughout Europe in the fifth century because he took up residence on top of a pillar. He began life as a shepherd boy in the mountains of northern Syria and joined a monastery at sixteen as a result of a revelation he had in a dream. Finding monastic life not sufficiently ascetic, he became a hermit and, in AD 423, he climbed a ten-foot pillar and stayed there. As the years passed, his pillars grew. The last thirty years of his life were spent on top of a fifty-foot pillar with only a railing and an iron collar round his neck, fastened by a chain, to prevent him from plunging to his death. His platform was so small that, though he could sit or kneel – and he constantly prostrated himself – he could not lie down. It was a prodigy of religious fervour that maintained him for so long in the face of the icy mountain winds and the pitiless summer sun. Meagre rations were carried up to him by ladder and rope by his fellow monks. Twice a week he celebrated Mass up there. Every day he preached to the crowd of pilgrims who gathered at the base of his column from all over Europe, even from remote Britain. It was literally an agony column, not only because of its discomfort, but because Simeon used to give advice from it. The assembled pilgrims would shout up their questions and he would answer, presumably at the top of his voice. He also pronounced on questions of religious policy and volunteered advice to the Emperor. But he scorned to enter into conversation with the many women who came as pilgrims. No women, not even his own mother, were allowed to approach

St Simeon's pillar, once fifty feet high, rests in the ruins of the finest Christian basilica in Syria

within the circle of stones that surrounded the pillar. He was one of the most renowned holy men of a holy time – buried with ceremony when he died in 459, at Antioch – and he inspired many imitators who also squatted on columns in the desert in succeeding centuries. You can still see his pillar – though there is not much of it left – at the abandoned hill-town of Qalaat Semaan (the fortress of Simeon) sixty miles north-west of Aleppo. After his death the pillar itself became a place of pilgrimage and, as with all sacred relics, everybody wanted a piece to take away. All that is left of its fifty feet is an oblong stump of weathered stone on a worn pedestal, no more than five or six feet high.

But what stands around it on this high, bare hillside is sublime. Because of the great numbers of pilgrims who continued to come, one of the finest and largest Christian churches to be seen in the East was built here in his memory. It is really four churches, arranged in the shape of a cross centering on the pillar, which stood in a domed octagonal space at the crossing point. There were enough pilgrims, many seeking baptism, to require four basilicas – though once again, women were not allowed to enter them. A large monastery was built for the numerous clergy and a town, with hostelries, sprang up on the slopes of the hill to accommodate the visitors. All this is now in ruins but the ruins are ravishing. The arches, columns, capitals, apses and octagons bear witness to an astonishingly ambitious and modern piece of architecture. You would expect them to date from Renaissance Rome, not from the primitive fifth century in such a remote place. The stone has weathered to subtle shades of sandy pink and gold. In the brilliant light, the arches cut hard-edged silhouettes against a sky of intense ultramarine. They create a space to wander in which is full of surprising harmonies and

out of every empty archway one glimpses vistas of the lonely, arid but magnificent moon-landscape of Northern Syria. To the north, the mountains of Turkish Anatolia swim in a haze. In other directions you can make out forlorn ruins and towers crowning distant crags – marking the sites of other 'ghost towns' of this once populous region. St Simeon on his pillar had a great view, though one imagines that his eyes dwelt mostly on that infinitely blue heaven, to which he wanted to be nearer. From the sight of this wilderness stretching as far as the eye can see, you can understand why men who lived amongst it turned to the most ascetic form of the spiritual life. Such spectacular surroundings challenge a man to do something equally spectacular to make his presence felt. The wind blows hard up here, the cold and the sunshine are both uncompromising. Sitting on the stump of the pillar, one can see a shepherd looking much like St Simeon must have looked, driving up the dusty road a flock of sheep the same colour as the golden brown stone. From the well beside the column an Arab comes to draw two buckets of fresh, clear water. If St Simeon returned today, he would find little had changed – not even the pilgrims. Even the Roman road, which ran nearby from Turkey into Syria and Palestine can be seen crossing the present road between them in excellent preservation. It marches across the countryside for nearly a mile, its massive blocks of limestone still dressed like a column of legionaries, so well laid that only shreds of the hardiest wild grasses have gained a foothold between them. People still walk it to reach the village that lies along its length and you could drive a car down it without much bumping.

Antioch, near the East Mediterranean coast, was part of Syria until it was annexed by Turkey from the French overlords of Syria in 1939. It was a great city in Roman times and it was there that Paul and Barnabas established the most important Christian church after Jerusalem. It was in Antioch that the adherents of the new faith were first called Christians, to distinguish them from the Jewish sects. It was at Antioch that the Gentiles first rallied to the faith and it is thought likely by some scholars that it was at Antioch that the Gospel of Matthew was written. After the sack of Jerusalem in AD 70, Antioch became the headquarters of St Paul and of the Christian church in the East. Since the twelfth century the patriarch has had his headquarters in Damascus and I met him near there in Saydanaya, one of the oldest convents in Christendom. Saydanaya is thirty kilometres north of Damascus on the road to Maloula and was founded in 547 by the Byzantine emperor, Justinian.

It was a Sunday morning and the courtyards of the convent were buzzing with churchgoers, visitors and nuns, the black habits of the nuns mingling with the *keffiyehs* of the visitors and the khaki of the Syrian soldiers who had climbed up to the convent's pinnacle to look at the view. The church was ablaze with twenty-seven chandeliers whose light suffused the building with the glimmer of gold – gold lamps, gold ikons, gold monstrances and the gold robes of the priest and patriarch as the Orthodox rite of Holy Eucharist took place from 8 a.m. to 10.30. To a Western visitor unused to Orthodox ritual, everything glitters like fairyland and the chandeliers, the gold and the chanting combine into a symphony of exotic piety. The priest, a huge and reassuringly cheerful man in his dazzling gold cope, appears at the gates of the altar sanctuary, raising his arms as if to embrace the congregation, then retreats behind the closed doors to celebrate the mysteries while lumps of unleavened bread are distributed to everybody. As the service

The Patriarch of Antioch, Elias Moawad

ends, the patriarch emerges grasping his silver-knobbed staff besieged by churchgoers who want his advice or blessing. He retreats for coffee and a cigarette in a room where he and the Mother Superior receive the Sunday visitors. Meanwhile the priest reappears in the church in a red and gold apron, rolling up his sleeves like a jolly blacksmith, ready to perform a couple of baptisms. Babies are baptized in the Orthodox Church by total immersion in a vast copper font and some take it better than others. Nuns bustle in and out bringing pans and buckets of warmed water. Godfathers and parents stand by the font holding candles. The priest swishes the baby face downwards through the water three times over, then holds the astonished child up at arm's length for a photograph. The ceremony also requires the baby to be marked on the forehead with holy oil and given a spoonful of sacred wine. Finally the relatives circle the lectern bearing an ikon amid clouds of incense and chanting, while a nun reads from the Testament at breakneck speed. To conclude this cheerful and triumphant ceremony, everybody in church is given baptismal presents of dates, sweets or chocolates.

Before the fuss of the baptisms has died down, the priest has changed back into his gold cope and put on his head-dress, concealing his pigtail (they do not cut their hair) and the bells are ringing for a wedding at which the patriarch himself will officiate. This was the wedding of an orphan girl brought up at the convent. She had been spotted and approved of by a visitor from Jordan. With typical Arab family feeling he had suggested her as an ideal bride for his brother, who was looking for one. The brother evidently agreed for here he was, looking suitably nervous in a bow-tie. 'They like to choose convent girls to marry,' confides one of the nuns, 'because they are well-educated and obedient.' The wedding begins traditionally with the un-church-like sound of high-pitched ululating cries from the women present, as they greet the bride's arrival at the church door. She is a dark, pretty girl in a white lace dress and veil provided by the nuns, looking pink with excitement and awe. She and her bridegroom are led up the aisle together by the priest, each of them holding candles tied with blue ribbons. While the priest recites the marriage service, the patriarch stands by the altar with folded hands, looking like an emperor in purple cope and gold stole embroidered with roses. But the sight that rivets the eye is his magnificent jewelled

The crowned patriarch reads the marriage service

crown with a cross of gold standing high on top of it. A crown like this needs a beard to balance it and the patriarch's beard is truly patriarchal, spreading, bushy and frosty white. The jolly priest can only boast of a grey tinge to his beard as yet. He intones a loud 'A-meen!' through the patriarch's prayers. The high point of the ceremony comes when the patriarch picks up two silver crowns which stand waiting on the altar, crosses them above the heads of, and then puts them on, the bridal couple. Then they all circle the altar in procession. The bridegroom's brother keeps his crown in place from behind while the bridesmaid does the

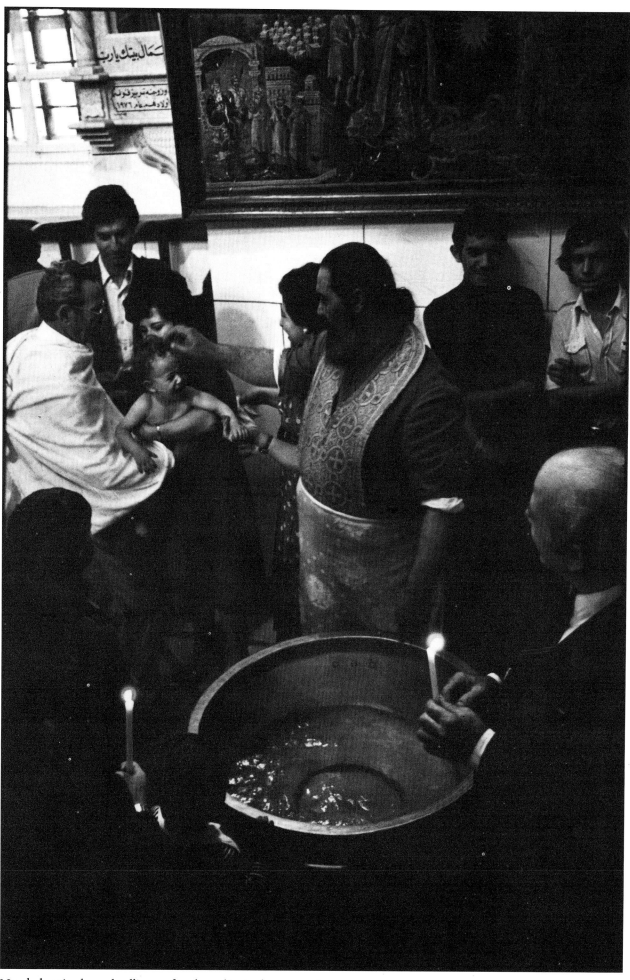

Newly baptized—and yelling—after three dips in the copper font

same service for the bride. The congregation, as at all weddings, want a closer look. They leave their seats and elbow their way up front near the altar, flashing pictures with their cameras, as the patriarch gives the couple his blessing. Then all of them pass by the couple to shake hands and hug them and their departure is marked with more ululating from the women. The pageantry of an Orthodox wedding is impressive but one is even more struck by its relaxed, human warmth and informality, a far cry from the chilly self-consciousness often found in Western churches. It is like a somewhat unruly class at school in which the patriarch and priest get on with their job, ignoring distractions and interruption.

The convent, perched on its rock like a fortress above the town, numbers about fifty sisters, whose work is to look after orphaned children, like this bride had been, who may be of all faiths and nationalities. The legend of its foundation is picturesque. The name Saydanaya means 'Our Lady' in Syriac but it also means a hunting place. The legend is that when the emperor Justinian was leading his troops towards Persia, he saw and pursued a beautiful gazelle which led him to this very hill. Before he could take aim, it was transfigured into an apparition of the Virgin, who stretched forth a hand and commanded him to build her a church on the spot. The Virgin Mary is still present at the convent. A little sacristy contains an ikon of her, said to have been painted by St Luke himself, which was brought there from Jerusalem by a monk. St Luke's paintings of the Virgin are fairly widespread – four exist. attributed to him. This one is credited with the power to cure women of infertility. Only a short while before, the King of Jordan's sister – a Muslim – had come here to pray before it and left her gold bracelet among the collection of personal jewellery and crosses that hang glittering before the

picture. She had duly given birth, the nuns said proudly. The picture hangs in a duskily lit, bejewelled little grotto, hung with immensely ancient, darkened ikons almost invisible in the carpeted darkness. Though the holy picture itself, known as El Chagoura, is scarcely visible behind its silver doors festooned with gold offerings, it is a mysterious and moving place full of whispered prayers. You have to take your shoes off at the door, Muslim fashion. A verse of Exodus over the entrance reminds you that this was not only a Muslim custom: 'Put off thy shoes from off thy feet for the place whereon thou standest is holy ground.'

After the wedding the patriarch's visitors approached, kissed his ring and pressed it to their foreheads before taking their seats around his reception room and being served by the nuns with coffee. Patriarch Elias Moawad, born in Beirut over sixty years ago, has been patriarch for eight years and, as such, head of a community of three and a half million Christians. Most of them are scattered through the Middle East but they also include the Orthodox communities of North and South America, to which he pays visits. Although his title comes from Antioch, this, it appears, is one of the harder places for him to go to since it was ceded to the Turks. He is at pains to point out, however, the degree of tolerance with which Arabs, both Muslim and Christian, normally live. together. Only the week before he had been to the funeral of a prominent Muslim sheikh. He had been the first Christian patriarch to visit Saudi Arabia and the first non-Muslim invited to attend the conference of Muslim heads of state at Lahore. Equally he had been to Washington to visit the President of the US and to attempt to enlighten the senators on Capitol Hill about the religious tolerance that can be found in Arab countries. 'Westerners have no understanding of the mentality of the Arabs,' he said. 'They just cannot understand that there are Christian Arabs, who speak Arabic. We are one community here. We have always lived together. My own teachers were all Muslims. Muslims come to pray at this shrine to ask help from the Madonna, who is recognized, like Jesus, in the Koran. A Muslim can marry a Christian wife and she does not have to convert to Islam. Why, in the Crusades, Muslims and Christians sometimes fought side by side against the invaders – it was an economic war more than a religious one.' This shrewd, intelligent man wearing a golden plaque, an *engolpion*, on his chest in place of a bishop's pectoral cross, drinking coffee, smoking cigarettes and conversing informally with the Mother Superior and his visitors in many languages, seems the acme of tolerance himself. 'Understand the Arabs and their religious tolerance,' he insisted again as we parted.

It is a lesson that one learns with surprise many times over in Syria which was once, like the Byzantine empire of which it formed part, a wholly Christian country and has never quite forgotten it. It is often assumed, out of ignorance, that Muhammad's teachings came as something completely foreign to Christians and their faith. In fact many of the chapters, or *suras*, of the Koran are very familiar to those brought up on the Bible. Muhammad's revelations encompassed many of the traditions, both Jewish and Christian, of the peoples of the area and built on them. How did he know of these? Muslim tradition tells how, as a young man, he paid several visits to Christian Syria accompanying the caravans which carried Eastern silks and spices from Arabia to Damascus. He came from a merchant family in Mecca and was taken on these journeys by his uncle – he had been left an orphan at the age of six. In particular, he is believed to have paid visits to Bosra, in the extreme south of modern Syria, where he met and held long conversations with a Christian monk called Bahira, who recognized his exceptional gifts and told his uncle that the young man was destined to become a prophet. It may well have been there, in Syria, about AD 590, that he learned of the still comparatively recent life and teachings of Jesus. When, at the age of forty at a cave outside Mecca, Muhammad had his vision of a celestial light and a being in the sky, he identified this being with the Biblical archangel Gabriel. The Koran is a record of the revelations from God that Gabriel ordered him to recite – he could not write – and the basic message was the same as that of the prophets who preceded him: Repent, for the Day of Judgment is at hand.

In 630 Muhammad led an army of 30,000 of his followers north from Arabia to near the Gulf of Aqaba to confront the major power in the area, the empire of Constantinople. The emperor was then Heraclius, who two years earlier had defeated and ejected the Persians from his domains in modern Iraq and taken back the sacred relic of the True Cross, which they had captured, and replaced it in Jerusalem. But the imperial army did not appear and Muhammad's army returned without a battle to Medina, where the Prophet, then over sixty, fell ill and died in 632. He had indicated the direction in which Islam was to expand.

In 634 his successor, the Caliph Abu Bakr (Caliph means 'successor'), issued the summons to a *Jihad*, or Holy War, and the Muslim armies advanced into Syria, Palestine and Iraq. The great Muslim general, Khalid ibn Walid, whom Muhammad called 'the sword of God', defeated the emperor's brother Theodore and his army west of Jerusalem and moved northward to besiege Damascus. After six months' siege the city surrendered in 635. The treaty Khalid made with the Damascenes was a model of toler-

The patriarch crosses the crowns above the bridal couple's heads

ance: he assured the people of Damascus of their lives and their goods, their churches and their city walls. 'No house will be pulled down or taken away from its owner. He promises them the protection of the Prophet, of his successors and of the faithful. He will do them no harm so long as they pay tribute.' A remarkable testimony to the conquerors was paid by a Christian bishop of Syria: 'The Arabs have become our masters but they do not war against the Christian religion. They protect our faith, respect our priests and holy men and make gifts to our churches.' This was a liberty that had not been enjoyed under Orthodox Byzantine rule, under which the Eastern Christians were persecuted for heresy.

The submission of Damascus was not the end of the war. Heraclius assembled an army at Antioch to drive the 'desert vermin' out of his colonies. Heavily outnumbered, Khalid withdrew from Damascus to the banks of the River Yarmuk, just south of the Sea of Galilee and, in August 636, the imperial army was routed by the warriors of Islam, inspired by Khalid's cry, 'Paradise is before you!' Syria was won at the battle of the Yarmuk. The emperor, in Antioch, abandoned his campaign and returned to Constantinople. Town after town surrendered without resistance to Khalid and the new Caliph, Omar, came to Syria to set up an Islamic state. Thanks to Omar's enlightened decrees, it was not a case of desert nomads plundering the land of settled farmers and merchants but of a peaceful occupation where prosperity continued. He forbade the soldiers to acquire land outside Arabia. Instead he levied taxes on landowners and a poll-tax on non-Muslims called the *jizya*, under which they were offered protection so long as they paid. The Christian civil service of the empire was left undisturbed and, for at least fifty years, continued to conduct administration in Greek.

Meanwhile the Muslim conquest continued in neighbouring territories. Jerusalem surrendered in 638 after a long siege. Iraq, then a Persian province, fell along with its wealthy capital Ctesiphon on the Tigris. Egypt followed, then parts of Persia itself. By 644, when Omar was struck down by the dagger of a Persian Christian prisoner in the mosque at Medina, the Arabs were masters of the Middle East.

It was during the caliphate of Omar that the sayings of the Koran were first collected into a book. They had been originally committed to memory by professional remembrancers and recited (Koran means 'recital'). Muhammad believed he was the mortal messenger entrusted with the word of God, which confirmed previous scriptures given to the Jews and the Christians but newly affirmed the oneness of God, and restated His commands. Such a message had a very powerful appeal in the seventh century when the Christians were divided into many sects, each in dispute over God's true nature. There was division between the Greek Orthodoxy, which dominated the Church, and the Syriac-speaking Semitic Christians. And the Eastern churches were themselves divided on the divine nature of Jesus – was he a man so perfect that he resembled God or was he God appearing as a man? The Nestorians – Bahira, who taught Muhammad, was a Nestorian – believed Jesus had two separate natures, divine and human. The Monophysites held that he had only one. Orthodoxy required belief in the doctrine of the Trinity, pronounced in the fourth century, that God was Three-in-One and One-in-Three. Against this theological confusion, Muhammad's message had the appeal of simple certainty: there was only one God, Allah the compassionate, the merciful. He had inspired a succession of messengers before Muhammad – Noah, Abraham, Moses, Joseph, David, Solomon,

Patriarch and Mother Superior, receiving Sunday visitors at Saydanaya

Job, Jonah and other prophets down to the most recent, John the Baptist and Jesus. They were all mortal men. The Koran insists on this at many points: 'Allah is but one God. Allah forbid that He should have a son!' 'Unbelievers are those that say "Allah is one of Three". There is but one God . . . The Messiah, the son of Mary, was no more than an Apostle: other Apostles passed away before him. His mother was a saintly woman. They both ate earthly food.' There was no equivocation in this message. There was simple certainty also in the five duties that Islam demands of the faithful: faith in one God, prayer, almsgiving, fasting in the month of Ramadan and pilgrimage to Mecca, if possible, once in a lifetime. It is a religion without priests – only teachers – with clearly stated rules on morals, law, and such practical matters as the treatment of women, divorce and diet, and with the promise of Paradise to come, except for the evil-doers. The success of the Arab conquests was followed by the swift conversion of many of the conquered peoples to Islam. Gradually Christians became minorities in Muslim communities.

As governor of Syria, Omar appointed Mu'awiya of the family of Omayya, which was to rule not only Syria but the whole Muslim world for a hundred years. Most of the early Caliphs met violent ends. After the murder of Omar came the assassination of his successor, Othman, stabbed to death while reading the Koran in his house at Medina in 656. Othman, a companion of Muhammad, was also an Omayyad and Mu'awiya was his cousin, with a duty to avenge his death. So began the civil wars that rent Islam for almost the rest of the century. They are extremely complex but the basic issue was the revolt against the Omayyads of the followers of Ali, the son-in-law of the Prophet. In choosing a Caliph, Ali had already been passed over three

times. Now the assassins of Othman offered him the title and he accepted it. As a result he was suspected of having consented to Othman's murder. Feelings were intensified when Othman's bloodstained shirt and the severed fingers of his wife, who had tried to protect him from the assassins, were exhibited in the mosque at Damascus. Muslim fought Muslim and, in 660, Mu'awiya was proclaimed as rival Caliph in Jerusalem, while Ali was acknowledged as Caliph in Kufa in Iraq, where he too was murdered the following year. Most Arabs then accepted the rule of the Omayyads but the schism which had started was to last until this day. The Shia sect of Islam, those who believed that Ali was the rightful first successor to the Prophet, as his nearest kinsman, continued as a distinct entity from the orthodox, or Sunni sect. They are the majority sect in Iran and Iraq and a sizeable minority in other Islamic lands. But at the time they were defeated. The capital of Islam moved to Damascus and there Mu'awiya ruled as Caliph for another twenty years – wisely and peacefully. His motto, when rebuked for using persuasion and gifts rather than force on the dissidents, was 'War costs more!' When he died at the age of eighty he introduced the hereditary principle to the Caliphate for the first time by insisting that his son, Yazid, should succeed him. At that point, Ali's son, Husain, then the only surviving grandson of the Prophet, raised a rebellion against Yazid. It was a hopeless cause. He advanced on Kufa, where his father had reigned, in the forlorn hope that it would rebel in his name. By the time he reached Kufa he had only a tiny force of seventy men and they died fighting fanatically against hopeless odds at Karbala on the tenth day of the month of Moharram in 680. This gesture of heroic martyrdom is commemorated with great mourning processions by the Shiites every year as if it happened yesterday.

The civil wars ended in 692 when the Syrians occupied Mecca itself and the head of the last of the pretenders to the Caliphate, Abdallah, was struck off and taken to Damascus, where it was presented to Mu'awiya's successor, Abd al-Malik. For the next twenty years the Omayyad empire expanded at breath-taking speed to West and East. The whole of North Africa and then Spain fell to the Holy War. Simultaneously, the Muslim armies conquered north-eastern Persia – including Bokhara and Samarkand – and reached the borders of the Chinese empire of the Tang dynasty. Other armies pushed down the Indus valley conquering what is now still Muslim Pakistan. The only place where the Arab advance was checked was Constantinople itself, which survived two sieges, the last of them in 718. Had the capital of the empire fallen, it is possible that Europe itself would have experienced Muslim rule, for the Arab armies in Spain were already raiding deep into France. Even so, the Arab empire at its limits, ruled from Damascus, was larger than the empire of Rome had been.

From 705 to 715, the Caliph Walid, who built the Great Mosque in Damascus, headed what was in effect a stable and efficient monarchy, unlike the old tribal societies of Arabia with which Islam had begun. Arabic had become the official language of government and the departments of state, or *diwans*, were staffed increasingly by Muslims. Mosques were built in every city, adorned with minarets in imitation of the first of these built on the Great Mosque. And Christians continued to worship unmolested provided they paid their taxes. The majority of the population of Syria under the Omayyads was still Christian but the Muslims were the ruling class.

The Omayyads came to a grisly end in 750 after a revolt by the Abbasids of Iraq, descendants of the Prophet's uncle, Abbas. The last Caliph of Damascus, Marwan, was beaten by them in battle, and killed in Egypt, where he had fled. According to the time-honoured ritual of those bloody times, his head was cut off and sent, with his Caliph's staff and ring, to Abu'l Abbas who was proclaimed Caliph in Kufa. Damascus and the Syrian fortresses surrendered without a fight. The graves of the Omayyads were broken into and their corpses were burned. The uncle of the new Caliph invited eighty Omayyad princes to be his guests and had them clubbed to death as they sat down to a banquet. Their broken and dying bodies were covered with leather aprons and the Caliph's uncle and his friends proceeded to eat their dinner using them as a table, accompanied by their dying groans. The centre of the empire moved to Iraq, where the new capital of Baghdad was built beside the ruins of Ctesiphon. The great days of Omayyad Damascus, which raised it to a glory equal to that of ancient Rome, were over.

The Latakia coastline

CRUSADER COUNTRY

SYRIA HAS 180 kilometres of coastline spreading north and south from its main port of Latakia, better known in classical times as Laodicea. It is a narrow coastal strip. Just inland and parallel to the coast runs a jagged mountain range rising from 3000 to nearly 5000 feet. It is the rain barrier which keeps the interior of Northern Syria as dry as a bone. The mountains are picturesque and for 200 years they formed the outposts of the first European colony to be established in Asia – the crusader kingdom which was called Outremer, literally 'Beyond the Sea'. The remains of the crusaders' castles, towers and look-outs spatter the crags of the mountain range of the Jebel Ansariya.

The ghostly remains of this romantic episode in history appeal to the imagination and add to the charm of the region and to its tourist potential, which is being exploited at high speed. There is a five-year plan to build 60,000 villas on the Latakia coast. Already it attracts over a million visitors a year and the tourists quickly out-run the accommodation. There are already 5000 villas, including one for the President, and 5000 more are under way, along with a new Meridien Hotel, rising like a pyramid along the coast road running north towards Turkey.

There is a lot to recommend this as the playground of Syria, above all the temperature, which remains in the low thirties centigrade in summer by contrast with the blistering forties experienced inland beyond the mountains. It is also a green and fertile area of orchards, orange groves and market gardens, giving way in the north to the evergreen pine forests on the foothills of the mountains. The last forest resort in Syria before you reach the Turkish frontier is Kassab, where the population is Armenian Christian and only Armenian is spoken, as it has always been. Forests are unknown except in this corner of Syria, which accounts for the popularity of the little resorts which are being developed there, among the soothingly odorous pines and the mountains sloping down to the sea. Latakia itself has the bustle of a Mediterranean port. It receives eighty to 120 boats a day which ride outside at anchor, twinkling at night, waiting for a berth in the harbour. The oil wharves and installations do not add to the attractions of the harbour but the coastal boulevard is lined with open-air restaurants with covered balconies where the fish is the best in Syria. One eats well here. Fish, vegetables and fruit abound. Latakia has the most French atmosphere in Syria, for it was the seat of French administration. There are wide boulevards, public gardens and avenues planted with flowers and oleanders and, here and there, traces of Roman times including a group of four columns and a Roman triumphal arch. Couscous, introduced by the French, is a local speciality. So is tobacco. Latakia is famed for its strong, dark tobacco and the largest cigarette factory in Syria puts it into Alhamra cigarettes, especially the strongest blend which is nearly black.

But most people who visit Latakia see it

The view from the ramparts of Saladin's castle

as a jumping-off point for the crusader castles of Outremer – still an adventure to reach because of their inaccessibility. There are three outstanding citadels: Marqab, which towers from a hilltop overlooking the oil port of Baniyas, south of Latakia; Saladin's Castle, hidden in the gorges inland; and, most complete of all, Krak des Chevaliers, perched above the gap in the mountains in the south-east leading to Homs.

Saladin's Castle is reached by turning from Latakia up a winding valley that is almost Tuscan in its domesticated paintability. The twists in the narrow road reveal new landscapes of contoured, green and brown terraced hillsides studded with olives and pencilled with cypresses like green fingers. Poplars rustle over streams in a golden light.

Finally the rocks break out on the skyline and the driving becomes precipitous. Emerging at the top of one dizzy ridge you look down into a gorge and up the wild slopes of the ravine opposite. Perched high above on the crags, like an eagle's nest, stands the castle, as arrogant and impregnable as any Romantic could wish.

It has only been designated Saladin's Castle – Qalaat Salah ad-Din in Arabic – since 1957. All through its long history as a fortress it was known as the castle of Sahyoun, which the Frankish crusader knights converted into the French form, Saône. It was first fortified by the Byzantines in their wars with the Arabs sometime before AD 1000. The crusaders occupied it in 1110 and built on it. Saladin, the hero of the Arab counter-attack, captured it from them in 1188. Even in 1965 it was impossible to cross the gorges which surround three sides of it except on foot or on horseback, by fording one of the fast-flowing streams at the foot of its cliffs. Now there is a narrow bridge and a road at a dizzy angle to enable you to drive across to the foot of the plateau on

which it stands. When you struggle up the other side you reach the castle by passing through a cleft between towering vertical faces of smooth, yellowish rock. In the middle of this passage-way stands the most extraordinary sight – an isolated, solitary needle of rock, like a rough-hewn obelisk, reaching exactly to the height of the cliff-faces on either side. Once you have been told why it matches them so exactly, the whole scheme fits into place. This narrow cleft is not the work of nature at all. It was dug out by human toil, leaving the pinnacle in the middle as the support for a drawbridge which lay across the chasm at the top. Having built their castle on the cliff-top surrounded on three sides by gorges, they dug through this narrow neck of rock which joined it to the rest of the plateau and made themselves an island in the air. If anyone approached from that side all they had to do was to raise the double drawbridge and cut themselves off completely. The task of cutting this great gash through sheer rock in the days before explosives is mind-bending. It is eighty-five feet deep, nearly fifty feet wide and nearly 500 feet long! How many man-hours of hard labour this represented for their prisoners or their slaves one can only shudder to imagine. But it is typical of the mentality of the crusaders. There was little that was noble, to our minds, about this religious war. But it inspired men to the most amazing feats of fortification, high up in these barren hard mountains.

What were they doing here? We left the history of Islam in the previous chapter at the height of its swift expansion into a world empire, stretching from Spain in the West to the Chinese borders in the East, which reached its zenith in about AD 750. Until the year 1000 the Muslim empire far surpassed in power and civilization anything in Western Europe, which was still a violent and illiterate battle-ground of raiding tribes. But by about 1090 the pendulum had swung the other way. The Franks, Germans and Normans had organized states. The Muslims had been driven out of Northern Spain, Sardinia, Sicily and Malta. The Mediterranean sea routes were open and Christian Europe responded to a call by the Pope for a great expedition to expel the Muslims from Palestine, the cradle of Christianity. The first Crusade set out from France and Germany in 1096, through Constantinople down into Syria and Palestine, with the slogan 'We shall slay for God's love the enemies of God in the East'. The Pope promised that all who fell on a Crusade were assured of going to heaven. St Bernard of Clairvaux urged 'murderers, rapists, adulterers, perjurers and all other criminals' to obtain saving grace by joining the fight. Those who did not hope to obtain entry to heaven at least hoped for plunder and estates in this world. There was a strong mixture of greed amid the religious enthusiasm. The first Crusade was a successful invasion of a disorganized land taken by surprise. Syria was in a state of anarchy with two brothers quarrelling for the throne amid racial feuds between Arabs, Turks and Kurds. Egypt was 'ruled' by a Caliph only five years old. The crusaders captured Antioch in 1098 and Jerusalem in 1099, soon followed by Tripoli, Beirut and Tyre, on what was then the Syrian coast. They set up the 'Latin kingdom of Jerusalem' under King Baldwin and a series of little states along the Syrian coast, ruled by Frankish counts and princes in Antioch, Tripoli and Edessa. The two main orders of knights, founded in Jerusalem, were the Knights Templar and the Knights Hospitaller (who originally ran a hospital in Jerusalem). They were in effect orders of military monks, who took vows of poverty, chastity and obedience, and fought under the sign of the Cross. The Knights Templar wore a red cross on their white surcoats, the Knights Hospitaller

Saladin's castle

a white cross on black. The castles they built or took over were organized rather like fortified, self-governing monasteries. The Crusades dragged on, with frequent pauses for a truce, for 200 years. But the knights never managed to penetrate Syria or capture an important Arab city, though they three times attacked Damascus, the last time in 1147–8. The second Crusade marched against the city under the King of France, Louis VII, and the Holy Roman Emperor,

Conrad, but were met by showers of arrows and stones from towers in the city's orchards. According to the Archbishop of Tyre who was with the army, 'Inside the walls lurked men with lances who could look out through small peep-holes and stab the passer-by from the side'. The army eventually retreated disheartened, leaving burial pits full of their dead men and horses, and never attempted to capture Damascus again. By then Arab resistance had revived under Nur ad-Din, who united Muslim Syria and established his rule in Damascus from 1154 to 1174. His successor was Salah ad-Din, known to us as Saladin, the greatest and most chivalrous general of his age.

Saladin is revered in Arab history as the man who re-conquered Jerusalem from the crusaders in 1187. He took it after a ten-day siege and is said to have wept at the sight of the crusader women mourning their dead. The following year he reached the castle of

Below the crusader castles the valleys are green and fertile.

Sahyoun, or Saône, which was garrisoned by the Knights Hospitaller. When you climb up into the castle you appreciate just what a tough nut it was to crack. Looking across the man-made chasm, over the top of the pinnacle, one sees on the farther side the little town which supplied the castle and whose inhabitants hurried over the drawbridge into the fortress in times of siege. It was from this side that Saladin bombarded the castle while his son led an assault army round through the gorges to attack it from the opposite side. How they got in is not easy to imagine when one looks down from those towering walls, but breach it they did. Saladin became its master – you can still see

his bath, which is under restoration. Indeed the plumbing is one of the features of the castle. There is an immense fresh water reservoir filled by rain-water guided down sloping surfaces to holes in its roof and you can see the courses of pipes running in pairs to the baths, one pipe for hot, one for cold. Saladin was a merciful conqueror. He did not kill the defending knights but freed them and their servants on payment of ten gold dinars for each man, five for a woman and two for a child. Saladin's capture of Jerusalem caused dismay in Europe and the third Crusade set out to win it back under the Emperor Barbarossa, King Philip of France and Richard the Lionheart, King of

England. They failed. Their army of 300,000 men got held up at the siege of Acre, whose Muslim defenders held out for two years before they were starved into surrender in 1191. Richard and Saladin regarded each other as knightly champions and models of chivalry. There is a story that when he saw the English king dismounted during the Battle of Jaffa, Saladin sent him a fresh horse. They eventually made a treaty of peace to last for three years and both went home to die. Richard went back to England a disappointed man. Saladin returned to Damascus in triumph, having won back all the lands conquered in the first Crusade except for the coastal strip and its fortresses. He died in the following year, 1193, worn out by fighting at the age of fifty-six. It is related that at his death his fortune consisted only of forty-seven dinars and one gold piece and when he was dying he sent for his standard bearer to carry, not his standard, but a piece of plain cloth on a lance at his funeral, to show that that was all he could carry out of this world.

Saladin's tomb lies just to the north of the Great Mosque in Damascus. There is nothing grand about it. It is suitably unpompous, in keeping with the austerity of its occupant. Inside the little mausoleum, with its grooved red dome, is the tomb, or rather two tombs. The ornate and heavy sarcophagus is modern and was presented as a gesture by Kaiser Wilhelm II of Germany, after he made a visit to the tomb before the First World War. He left his monogram on a gold lamp hanging over the grave. The other tomb is said to be that of Saladin's secretary.

Saladin's descendants, the Ayyubid dynasty, ruled Syria for another sixty years. But it was another dynasty, the Mamluks, who finally expelled the Crusaders under a Sultan nicknamed 'the panther' – Sultan Beybars, in Arabic. The Knights Hospitaller were still holding out in their castles, above all in the most massive and best preserved of all, the castle called Krak des Chevaliers, which even Saladin did not attempt to storm.

Krak des Chevaliers derives its name from the Syriac word for a fortress – Kark – and thus means 'fortress of the Knights'. It lies on the slopes of the gap between the two coastal mountain ranges, the Jebel Ansariya to the north and the Lebanon mountains to the south. It is called the Homs Gap, the only river valley that connects the interior of Syria with the sea and therefore of great strategic importance. There was a Kurdish castle here before the crusaders came but the greater part of it was built by the knights, who finished it in 1170 and held out in it for a hundred years. T. E. Lawrence, who studied crusader castles and wrote a book about them while he was still at Oxford, called Krak 'perhaps the most wholly admirable castle in the world' and anyone who dreamed of castles in childhood must exclaim, on seeing it, '*That's* what I mean by a castle!' It sits four-square at 2000 feet on a hilly peninsular jutting out into the valley and its roundness at every turretted corner is its charm. It not only looks massive but human and fun to live in – it could be the model for a child's sandcastle. The turret-shaped bastions and towers turn from limestone white to sandy brown as they curve around. Bushes and grasses growing from the sheer walls relieve the monotony of the stone. The whole structure floats like a great ship in the air against the mountainscape of purple-brown hills, wrinkled and bare as elephant hide. The best place to take it in as a whole, after you have struggled up the rugged road from the Homs-Tartus highway, is to go on climbing, passing the main gate, and up the hill beyond the farther, western face of the castle. Here, as the sun sinks behind you, it glows to perfection.

One way of seeing the castle is to walk round the ramparts of the outer walls, looking inwards. The inner fortress rises from the inner moat which is fed by an aqueduct running into the castle from the hillside. The inner walls rise at an angle steeper than the sides of the pyramids, broken by great round towers, the biggest of which was the lodgings of the Grand Master of the knights' order. From his windows he could survey the interior of the castle courtyards as well as look out on the valleys of the pass.

When you enter through the main postern gate, you realize how ingenious a piece of military architecture this is. A vast vaulted passage climbs sideways up shallow steps into the castle, broad enough to take the knights on horseback but full of defence points from which it could be bombarded in case invaders got into the castle this way. It comes out under further gateways and portcullises into an inner courtyard which has the atmosphere of a college quadrangle. Leading off the courtyard is the great hall, eighty feet long and vaulted with pointed arches, where the meetings of the Chapter of the Knights Hospitaller were held. The castle was governed by the Chapter Knights under their Grand Master, meeting in council as a sort of Castle Parliament at which ordinary knights were not permitted to speak. There are two other huge halls, the 'Hall of the Massive Pillars', like a forest of low columns inside, which housed the refectories and kitchens, and the 'Hundred and Twenty Metre Hall' (for such is its vast length) which stored the provisions. The castle carried enough supplies to last its 2000 men for a five-year siege. Also opening off the courtyard is a knights' chapel, an austerely simple interior, with a stone Muslim pulpit placed against one pillar, dating from the capture of the castle when the chapel was turned into a mosque.

It was captured by Beybars, the panther, after, not a five-year but, a five-week siege in 1271. Krak was cracked from the south side, where its promontory joins the hill behind. The large square tower in the outer walls was built by the Arabs to replace the breach they made in the walls. It is a mystery that the great fortress, 'the bone in the throat of the Muslims', which had defied capture for a hundred years, did not stand out longer. There is a story that Beybars forged a letter from the Grand Master, then in Tripoli, instructing the Hospitallers to surrender, but this seems doubtful. The surviving knights were allowed to withdraw under safe-conduct back to Tartus on the coast and there you can see the cathedral where they celebrated their last mass in 1291 before putting to sea. This church had once witnessed the full mediaeval brilliance of the Crusades at the wedding there of Alice of Champagne, widow of the King of Cyprus, to the Prince of Antioch, Bohemond. The entire court of the Kingdoms of Outremer assembled in their silks and brocades and jewels. But the bride was in tears – she had wanted to marry a handsome Muslim emir. The King of Jerusalem had hurriedly put a stop to that and substituted a more suitable Christian prince. But one wonders how often during the frequent lulls in the fighting, the two warring sides fraternized and even got romantically entangled. Richard the Lionheart considered marrying his sister to Saladin's brother as a means of ending the war by a political alliance. At last the long war of conquest and reconquest, plunder and religious fanaticism petered out in exhaustion. The crusaders left Tartus – then called Tortosa – and in 1302 the last of them stole away from their final outpost, the little island of Arwad, opposite the port. They retreated steadily westwards, becoming Knights of Rhodes and then Knights of Malta, from where Napoleon finally evicted them.

ALEPPO

THE CITADEL of Aleppo sits astride its ravaged rock, which rises like a humpbacked whale in the centre of the city, burying who-knows-what layers of civilization beneath it. This is one of the sights of Syria – more dramatic than any view that Damascus can offer. The citadel on top of the rock was big enough for the entire population of the town to retreat within it in earlier centuries. For much of their early history, Aleppo and Damascus were the capitals of separate and rival kingdoms. The two cities are rivals still. Though only 350 kilometres apart, they are markedly different in appearance, in atmosphere and in the character of their citizens. Aleppo has a brisk, northern, energetic tang in the air. It is compact, a town with a centre where the streets and squares and gardens (far better laid out than Damascus) are lively and full of evening strollers. It is a clean, hard-working place that also knows how to relax. And it has a great civic pride. An Aleppo citizen has no doubts that he lives in the most interesting and agreeable city in Syria. And no visitor comes away without the town leaving a lasting impression of its spirited atmosphere. Part of what makes Aleppo feel special is its solitude in the midst of the arid, brick-red steppe that stretches for miles all around it. In every direction there is flatness and emptiness. To the east there are no trees for 150 kilometres until you reach the Euphrates. To the south, towards Hamah and Homs, stretch miles of monotony. To the north west lie the jagged dry mountains of the pillar-squatting saints and the 'ghost-towns' left as abandoned ruins since the crusaders' times. Marooned in its high, dry plains, in a shallow bowl of fertility, Aleppo bursts on the view with a sense of astonished relief. No sullen, mud-baked town but a large bowlful of stone, of palest silver, gold and rose-tinted grey, jumbled, crooked, domed and minareted. And dominating it all is this awe-inspiring hump of rock, thrust up above the brick-coloured horizon, tooth-edged with fortifications and a single minaret like a pointing finger.

A Russian merchant making his way there in 1465 noted that the citadel could be seen when he was three days' march away. The rock it stands on has been fortified since the days of the Hittites and Assyrians. On top of their remains were piled Greek, Roman and Byzantine fortifications. But the present Arab citadel dates from 1183 when Saladin, the scourge of the Crusaders, gave Aleppo to one of his sons, Malik es-Zaher. As Sultan of Aleppo he rebuilt the castle and made himself a palace inside it.

How old is Aleppo, or Haleb as it is called in Arab history? It is keenly disputed between Aleppo and Damascus which of them is the oldest continuously inhabited city in the world and neither of them will accept the other's claim. There is no definitive answer. The earliest mention of Aleppo on tablets was in 1900 BC. Before that, its history is guesswork. Not far away was the city-kingdom of Ebla which was destroyed in 2250 BC and whose records are silent about Aleppo. Those who favour the claim of Damascus to be the elder have this evidence to put forward. But at that epoch the gaps in our knowledge swamp the few

Inside Aleppo's citadel: a mosque framed by a door in the fortifications

islands of recorded history. We know nothing about the kingdom of Yamhad which was centred on Aleppo in the third millennium, 3000–2000 BC. The evidence is buried beneath the citadel and the bustling town and nobody is likely to be allowed to dig it up to satisfy our curiosity. There is a persistent legend that Abraham halted at Aleppo on his journey to the South and, so the story insists, milked his cows on top of the citadel mound. If he did, it is certain there had already been a fortress there for several centuries before his time, which is dated, and disputed, among scholars at between 2000 and 1400 BC. Aleppo was a crossroads on the northernmost trade route from the Euphrates and the Tigris and the route north from Arabia. Though those routes are obsolete it is still an important merchant city, with the biggest and best-preserved covered *suq* in Syria.

What we see today are the massive remains of a masterpiece of Arab military architecture, more square-cut than the castles of the crusaders, who never dared attack it, and every bit as ingenious in its defences. The only way in, across the great sixty-foot moat and up the sheer limestone slopes of the castle mound, is through the great gate built by Saladin's son, the Emir Zaher, and up the great stone stairway built on a colonnaded bridge across the moat. The steps are filled in the middle by ramps, like a pair of stone tram-lines, to enable wheeled traffic to get up them. I watched stone for restoration work being hauled up by donkey-drawn cart, just as it must have been eight centuries ago, except that in this case the poor donkey has the assistance of a winched cable to stop the cart from running away. Thus you reach the first of the great gates into the bastion, overlooked by arrow-slits

and overhung by stone look-outs and protruberances from which anyone foolhardy enough to try to storm the bridge would be caught in a hail of stones and boiling oil. The same welcome awaited them inside the gate. The high-vaulted entrance passage turns corners at sharp angles – and at each corner great iron gates could be closed to trap them, while from high above more grilles and slits would be waiting to disgorge more boiling oil. Indeed, keeping oil on the boil must have been one of the key responsibilities in the garrison. But for all its fierce and forbidding grandeur, the citadel is relieved by Arabic decoration. The outside window-embrasures are picked out in bands of coloured stone and carved strips and patterns. A wide band of inscription runs right round the great square block of the keep and the massive inside doors have lintels carved with lions and dragons.

As you climb inside, emerging into the daylight, you realize this was not just a castle, it was a small city, in which there were huge store-rooms for siege provisions, dungeons for prisoners, wells, shops, a little Byzantine church with a low pudding-basin dome, and the remains of the mosque built by Zaher crowning the summit with its minaret, which you can climb, rather hazardously, to look out over the entire city. It is also a shattered ruin. It was conquered, soon after the Saladin era, by the Mongols in 1260. Later, in 1400, Tamerlane, a Turk, led the second Mongol invasion. He slaughtered 20,000 of Aleppo's inhabitants, and made piles of their severed heads. The ruins, sprawled where they fell, are left untidied and unswept up in the Arab manner. You can be guided or you can roam freely at will – and at your own risk. You can sit on the ramparts taking coffee in the sunshine while the busy city peeps its horns like a beetle-race below. At the edges there is nothing to stop you from tumbling down

The barber at work

the steep sides of the mound or falling into the holes designed for pouring boiling oil through. It is an adventure playground of a castle and perilous to explore without a goat's sure-footedness.

The only major restoration is of part of the Sultan's palace, built by Saladin's son and enlarged under the Mamluks, the Egyptian dynasty that succeeded Saladin's and stood up, first to the Mongol invasions and then to Tamerlane the Turk in 1400. The Mamluk throne-room has been recreated by Syrian craftsmen much as it must have looked in the time of our own Tudors and Elizabethans. It is an interior as rich as anything that the period has to show, with coloured columns, coloured glass, carved and painted roof-beams and beautifully dec-

Traveller in suiting

orated ceiling panels taken from the old houses of Aleppo merchants. One hopes that more of the citadel will be restored with such loving care.

To the west of the citadel, between the mound and the remains of the city walls, stretches the amazing mediaeval *suq* of Aleppo, a labyrinth of stone-roofed streets winding in an intricate pattern which, if stretched out, they say, would run for eight miles. From the heights of the citadel one looks out over their ancient roofs adorned with chickens in coops and sprouting enough grass from between the stones to graze the occasional goat and sheep, which no doubt ends its life on a butcher's stall one storey below. When you descend from the citadel, you will see the tomb of the man

The arches of Aleppo's cotton *suq*

Aleppo's pale stone townscape set off by its lush gardens

Aleppo sits in a bowl surrounded by bare steppe and solitude

The bustle of the streets flows round old merchant houses

The *suq* of the coppersmiths where hammers rise and fall in an anvil chorus

Early-morning vegetable market beneath the citadel

Visiting a street-side cemetery

The nut seller on his perch

who built it, the Emir Zaher, son of Saladin, in a small domed building nearby which is a *Madrassa*, or Islamic school of theology. To the west lies a network of little streets, bursting with traders, which gives access to the labyrinth of the covered *suq*. It is a much better organized *suq* than the one in Damascus. Everything has its place – meat, vegetables, spices, cotton, rope, cloth, leather, hardware – and is displayed with great effect against these thick stone passageways with vaulted arches that wind in every direction like the subterranean passages of an enormous colosseum. It is every child's picture of an oriental bazaar. The bales of materials glow like Christmas decorations piled up in those vaulted openings. Women with babies are shopping, pulling out roll after roll of vibrating colour and pattern, crumpling the cloth with their hands and putting on that bored and listless expression that women often assume when they are going to bargain for it.

In the meat *suq* you need a strong stomach, for carcases are prepared on the spot. You may have to make way for a man with two sheep carcases over his shoulders, their intestines still slithering and wobbling inside. Sheep's heads are being filleted on the stalls. A man thrusts his hand into a heaving sack and yanks out a live pigeon to offer you. In all this hubbub, donkeys are being loaded and driven and little vans are squeaking to be let through the crowd. The people are often as colourful as the goods. Here you will see a large, swarthy, gipsy-like woman trader in a glittering gold shawl over a dress and pantaloons of bright blue and red, the whole effect topped with a white head-dress. You pass through an archway and turn another right angle and the whole character of the place has changed again: it may be the rope *suq* with its peculiar smell of hemp, where there are stalls piled with nothing but balls of string and thread

in dazzling red, blue or violet, as well as white. There are reels and bobbins and twists of string, a kite-flyer's paradise. There are great bricks of soap and sacks of sulphur, for sheep dipping. There are old-fashioned besom hand brushes, natural and soft with plaited straw handles, hung up from a pole like the drooping fronds of a yellow palm tree. There are baskets, round and bulbous, shaped like tea-cups, coffee-cups or great Ali Baba jars, hanging overhead like enormous clusters of fruit. Turn another corner and a fragrant but biting bouquet of smells assails your nostrils – it is the spice *suq*. Sacks and trays are piled up on the stalls and on the ground, full of nutmeg and coriander and cumin seeds and peppercorns and the aniseed with which arak is flavoured. There was a wizened stall-holder in his white skullcap with his head laid on the counter, asleep among his aromatic sacks and tins. Among the more curious commodities is dried henna, which is boiled like tea to decorate the palms of women who are attending a wedding, according to old country custom. The bride, her mother and the girls who attend her will go to sleep clutching henna in each palm, bound up with stockings, to turn it red. Designs are made with threads, which will last for about three months, as an aid to the bride's attractions. In another part of the *suq*, you enter a wintry wonderland of raw cotton and wool in bursting bales of dazzling white, filling the air with their slightly oily aroma. The stone recesses are filled with softness like falls of new snow. At least the merchants have something comfortable to sit on or lean against, while black-veiled women with hooked noses try a handful of this bale or that – do they take it home to spin themselves? Meanwhile young boys are beating fleeces of new wool, laid out on the cobbled passages, with long wiry whips and the donkeys which carry the bales to and

The toolmaker and his apprentice

The key-maker's shop

The old wooden houses of Aleppo—a study in lattice-work and shutters

from the market wait in patient lines tethered to the outer wall.

Jumbled in amongst the *suqs* are the *khans*, or caravanserais, where for centuries past the foreign merchants stayed or took up residence with their goods and their horses and camels. They open off the *suqs* through great stone doorways leading into courtyards, in which trees grow and animals are still tethered among sacks and bales. The *Khan al-Goumrok*, which means the 'customs caravanserai', dates from the seventeenth century and was the headquarters of the British Company of the Levant. The French, the Dutch and the Venetian traders also lived in the *khans* and so did their consuls.

In the *Khan al-Nahassin* you can see, and ask to visit, the former Venetian consulate dating from the fifteenth century. It is now known as the house of Monsieur Poche, who has lived there for many years as the Belgian consul and president of the Archaeological Society. Dr Poche's house is the oldest continually inhabited house in Aleppo. The *khan* it stands in (the *Khan al-Nahassin* means the 'coppersmiths' caravanserai') was built by the Venetians in 1539 to protect their traders and their goods and to house their consul, who negotiated transactions. The big courtyard, with a fully-grown tree in it, was for exhibiting their goods, the ground floor was for warehouses and stabling, while they lived upstairs alongside their consul. The narrow gate into the courtyard, big enough to admit a train of camels one by one, was shut at sunset to keep out intruders. The courtyard is nowadays mainly occupied by shoemakers and their strings of shoes.

When Venice fell to Napoleon at the end of the eighteenth century, the consul's sixteen-roomed house was taken over by Dr Poche's great-grandfather, the Austrian director of a trading company, who married the daughter of the last Venetian consul. The

family has lived there ever since. Dr Poche, born there in 1895, became a physician, and served as Belgian consul in Aleppo from 1939. As a scholar, historian and archaeologist, he has maintained the house almost exactly as it has been for four centuries and filled it with antiques from old Aleppo and Syrian archaeological treasures. Requests to see over his historic home can be made through the archaeological society at the Aleppo Museum.

Opening off one of the central alleys of the *suq* is a doorway leading down some steps into what looks us though it might be a large green-tiled barber's saloon. It is a Turkish bath or *Hammam* – more than a bath, an experience to be recommended. This time-honoured but efficient form of refreshment from the stifling heat of summer is a ceremonial occasion, at a very reasonable price.

The main hall is a relaxation room lined with divans on raised platforms where you undress, are swathed in a towelling robe and given built-up wooden sandals in which to negotiate the hot tiled floors. The steam rooms are a murky labyrinth of varying temperatures where you can linger as long as you can stand it. Then comes the massage, performed by a squat powerful Syrian who might well be an executioner out of an Arabian Nights tale in his turban and loincloth. He wastes no time on words. With a peremptory gesture he sits you down and douses you with water from a bucket, then forcefully loofahs you all over with soap. At intervals he administers a resounding slap to indicate it is time to turn over. On returning to the main hall you are wrapped up in towels and a head-cloth by an attendant. You sit cross-legged on one of the divans and your knees are covered with what looks like a table-cloth while hot sweet tea is served to you. Sitting there, alongside the other clients, smoking, looking like an Arab, feeling deliciously clean and rested, you are fit to face the heat and bustle of the *suq* again. Just along the alley-way near the door is a thoughtfully placed soft-drink bar where they will prepare fresh carrot juice, banana, orange, lime or any combination of them on the spot. The soft-drink bars are a feature of Aleppo, remarkable for their excellence and cleanliness. In a Muslim country the public bars are devoted to fresh fruit drinks and nuts, served in separate establishments. The nut bars display their huge variety, including the most excellent pistachios, on circular drums and you sit at a counter to eat them. Arabs take nuts as seriously as Europeans take drinking alcohol. Along the same streets you will find cooked meat counters ready to slice and serve tit-bits of smoked tongue and sausage for enjoyment on the spot. It is possible to eat very well on the streets. In the hotels and cafés Aleppo beer is served – the best beer in Syria, richer and more hop flavoured by far than the beer of Damascus. Aleppo is also famed for producing the best shish kebab in Syria. Most of these refreshments, along with the squad of shoe-shine men with their beautifully kept brass shrines set out on the pavement, are to be found near the Clock Tower, a landmark in the town centre which is always vibrating with life. There are also shoe-shine shops where the walls are lined with big chairs, like a barber's, and the customers read newspapers and chat with their neighbours. On many of the older inhabitants' faces you will see the 'Aleppo mark' – an indented pock-mark, the size of a small coin, on the cheek or neck. Until a few years ago, the town's drinking water was drawn from the river, in which lives a microscopic worm which causes this skin blemish. It was harmless but noticeable – other Syrians can always tell an Aleppo citizen by its presence. Now that the water supply has been changed it is dying out.

No one who likes things symmetrical should go wandering around old Aleppo. Its chief charm is that everything is wonky. The minarets are wonky, the verandas are wonky, the dust-encrusted shutters are wonky, the gateways are wonky, the surviving stretches of the city wall are wonky and are used to prop up thickets of wonky-walled houses. It is as if the city had been given a good shake by one of its earthquakes, was in the very act of preparing to fall down but, at the last moment, decided to go on standing. The antique is too commonplace to be venerated or displayed in Aleppo. Many of its oldest buildings and archways are scarcely visible behind the clutter of workshops, shacks and sheds that have piled up against them – wonkily, of course – in the course of time. An outstanding example of ordered chaos is the *suq* of the coppersmiths to the north of the citadel, off the *Rue al-Qawaqbi*. You can hear it long before you see it . . . its presence is announced by an anvil chorus of the clonking and pinging of hammers. You reach it through a gateway into what appears to be waste ground, piled with tips of rubbish and old metal. Then you realize this is in fact a metal factory that looks as though it has not been cleared up for centuries. There is a long, winding lane leading away between two lines of ramshackle workshops, whose frontages have been burnt black by the coppersmiths' forges. They are really a series of holes in the wall – the ground-floor, open to the street, being the forge and the upper storey the store-rooms, where you can see huge and venerable pots and jars of black metal gathering cobwebs. Except for the slight aid of naked electric bulbs in the dark interiors and the roaring of gas in the forges, nothing has changed since the great-grandfathers of these coppersmiths worked here. The smiths sit on three-legged stools along the edge of the street. Look down it and you

The village of Maloula, clinging to the cliff-face, with its powder-blue houses

Below, right: St Simeon's Basilica

The Great Mosque's minaret, seen through the columns of the Roman temple, its magnificent
mosaic and its great courtyard

Latakia: the holiday coast and the verdant valleys above the town

Krak des Chevaliers

Saladin's Castle: the pillar of rock cut out
by human hands to support the double
drawbridge; (inset) the ramparts, the keep
and a defender's eye-view of the approaches

Below: the vaulted reservoir for fresh water

Aleppo's citadel, astride its ravaged rock in the centre of the city, is one of the sights of Syria

The citadel, protected by a sixty-foot moat and steep limestone slopes, is only approachable via the bridge and through the huge fortified gate built by Saladin's son. Inside the fortifications lies virtually a miniature city into which the inhabitants could retreat during a siege

The keeper of the water wheels in the ancient City of Hamah

The bootblack's shrine

Aleppo cotton merchants in their *suq*

The craftsman and his works

will see long-headed hammers rising and falling on their anvils like the instruments of a symphony orchestra, beating bowls and trays and cooking pans and coffee pots in an eternal orchestral 'tutti' – fortissimo. The coppersmiths' trade is still a handcraft. It can hardly be mechanized, though you will see lathes spinning, polishing and burnishing copper geysers into glowing cylinders as bright as curved mirrors. I was invited to sit down on one of the low, three-legged stools and try my hand at hammering a copper pan, crinkle-edged from the firing, into a smooth-sided bowl. The trick is to hit hard on every other stroke of the hammer and use the rebound to help the intervening alternate stroke. Even so, ironing out the crinkles of even a modest bowl is hard on the wrist. There is also the thumb holding the object to consider, constantly, for it is harder still on that. It is also hard on the hearing. I was one of a group of twelve men outside this particular workshop and the din we kicked up was deafening . . . though, like people living beside a railway, they get used to it. But it is a cheerful, open-air trade, better by far than working in some dark Satanic mill. The sun shone, donkeys and veiled women passed, even a white butterfly wobbled by. The craftsman who was teaching me began as a boy, like his father and grandfather before him. There beside him was a boy who looked no more than twelve years old, who sat down for a burst of expert hammering, training to succeed his father. And the products of their trade are satisfying to create and hold. I came away with a bowl, silver finished, whose beaten pewter surface is a pleasure to handle and to behold. It was sold by weight, after the necessary bargaining. The handcraftsman still rules in Aleppo. Around the courtyard of the Great Mosque in the centre of the covered *suq*, workshops are bustling with the manufacture of a wide variety of metal implements:

A rest from beating the fleece

one workshop makes nothing but door handles; another big funnels and churns; some specialize in gouges, coils of copper wire, meat-hooks and kebab skewers. In the midst of this is a shop full of cane chairs, such as Van Gogh painted, which are woven and plaited on the kerbside in front of it.

The most mysterious quarter of Aleppo is the Jedeide district. This is a maze of limestone town-houses, mostly built and occupied by Christian Armenians, who have lived here since the sixteenth century. It is criss-crossed by narrow stone passageways, passing under great stone vaults and archways and leading unexpectedly into court-

Coppersmiths beating in unison

yards with fountains and flowering creepers. Here, there is the feeling of a cathedral town. The doorways, reached up flights of steps, are set in carved stone surrounds. Here and there you will see a window as ornate as that of a church in its carving, and at roof level you will see more carved decoration and the occasional gargoyle. It is a unique quarter, an architectural tour by day and an atmospheric journey of adventure by night. Dusk shrouds these long perspectives of archways and peaceful, cloistered paths, within a few yards of the bright lights of the shopping streets and the fascinating recesses of the antique shops.

Aleppo has a town centre that has taste and dignity, all the better for being the taste of the late nineteenth and early twentieth century. One of its curiosities is the Hotel Baron in the Rue Baron, a survival from the spacious days of oriental travel, the Raffles of Aleppo. It has played host to archaeological expeditions since before the First World War. T. E. Lawrence stayed here on Sir Leonard Woolley's expedition to Carcemish, just over the Turkish border. Between the wars, aviators like Lindbergh stopped over here on the air races to Australia. The interior is still living in that era, happily unimproved, and it was here that the hotel's most famous resident, Agatha Christie, came to stay during one of her husband's archaeological digs in the thirties. She came by the Orient Express via Istanbul, on the last extension of the line which terminates at Aleppo. The train – alas, no longer with us – was immortalized in the book she wrote here, *Murder on the Orient Express.*

That is not the only mystery that the Aleppo region has sponsored. Another is the mystery of the hiding places of the golden hamster. All the golden hamsters in the world – and there are hundreds of thousands kept as pets and laboratory animals – are descended from a single female captured near Aleppo in 1930. The hamster is a semi-desert rodent and the dry, stony highland around Aleppo is the only place where it is known to live as nature intended. But so secretive are hamsters in the wild that no others had been caught for nearly one hundred years. In 1839 the only previous example known was exhibited at the Zoological Society of London as a newly-discovered species. The 1930 female was pregnant with twelve young and the entire world population of tame hamsters was bred from them, at least until 1971, when eight more were caught. A further two were captured in 1978. All of them from the vicinity of two villages, called Benjamin and Blat. One marvels at the way these shy animals have kept their privacy underground, inviolate from man. An animal expert working for the UN told me that he had spent long periods trying to trap them above ground by pouring water down their holes in the hope that they would come out to shake themselves dry. The hamsters were too wily or too cautious: not one appeared. The profession of hamster-trapping seems certain to remain a very small and unprofitable one. It is surprising to learn, by the way, that lions also flourished in these desert foothills of Northern Syria until the last century. In ancient times there were even elephants on the banks of the Euphrates.

The only lions to be seen now are the great stone beasts of the Aleppo Museum which, along with the Damascus National Museum, is one of the sights of Syria. 'The Dawn of Civilization' is an overworked phrase but looking at the great stone beasts that guard the Aleppo Museum you feel very close to it indeed. The city-states of the Syrian desert were contemporary with the early cities of Mesopotamia. Practically the whole of the civilized world was crammed into this neck of land between the Syrian coast and the two great river basins, the

Euphrates and the Tigris. The chief Syrian cities among them were Mari, Tell Halaf, Ugarit and Ebla. (Chapter two deals with these civilizations and their role in Syrian history.)

The five great beasts guarding the museum entrance porch used to guard the entrance to the Palace-Temple of Tell Halaf in extreme north-eastern Syria. They are fantastic and disconcerting in form and appearance because they stare at you with eyes as white as china eggs, set in the black basalt of which they are carved. It is not a pretty sight. In the centre the god Hadad, god of the weather, stands on the back of a bull. To either side of him a god and goddess are standing on lions with massive upper and lower fangs. To either side of them are two sphinxes. The tall cylindrical head-dresses of the gods rise above their stern, bearded, staring faces like chimneys, reaching the wooden porch that shields them from the sun, as it did twenty-eight centuries ago outside the palace of this Aramean kingdom. These are not old by Syrian standards. Inside, you step back forty-four centuries when you enter the rooms devoted to Ebla and to Mari. Ebla, famed for its library of clay tablets, has not so far yielded much in the way of works of art. There is a cistern, covered with bearded elders holding hands rather comically, as if they were singing 'Auld Lang Syne'. There are little ceramic figurines and bits of gold jewellery, but the real interest is the tablets, shaped like television screens and ruled in rectangular columns of script. Some are blackened by the fire which destroyed the wooden library shelves that held them in 2250 BC. They are now being translated, tablet by tablet, 4200 years later.

The Mari exhibits are far more striking to the uninstructed eye. Who are these bald-headed, topless men with huge eyes and ears, wrapped in heavy sheepskin skirts with their hands clasped unctuously in front of them? They are the princes and priests of Mari, who shaved their heads and were represented with outsize eyes and ears to impress on their primitive subjects that, like gods, they could see and hear everything. One hand clasping the other denotes a priest. One hand clasping the wrist denotes a prince. One of the priests' duties was to make love to the girl servants of the temple – a duty that also fell to the strongest men of the city, decided by wrestling contest. Mari was a trading kingdom at the extreme south-east corner of Syria near the Euphrates on the border with Iraq. It flourished contemporaneously with Ebla, whose King Dagan conquered it. The most impressive and beautiful statue from Mari is the Goddess with a Flowing Vase. She stands all alone commanding a gallery with her vase tipped forward to gush water. Her hair is plaited and coiled on her head and hangs down her back. She is wonderfully preserved down to every toe – an amazing survival from 1800 BC, and one of the most beautiful statues from the ancient world. Another oddly touching piece of statuary is of two lovers sitting side by side, wearing sheepskins. They have lost their heads since the third millennium but you can see how he has leaned across to grasp her right arm with his left hand. It is strange to see them sitting there so demurely in this affectionate pose after nearly 5000 years.

Almost a thousand years passes when you step into the room devoted to Ugarit, the city-state that flourished just north of Latakia from around 1450 BC, where the first alphabet was invented. Here was discovered real buried treasure – works of art in gold – for Ugarit was a rich city, the main Syrian port of its era and a station on caravan routes from all over the Near East to the Mediterranean. Among these treasures is a large and priceless golden bowl

The citadel gate, its arch carved with writhing dragons

ALPHABET D'UGARIT

UGARIT	Alph. Latin	Alph Arabe	UGARIT	Alph. Latin	Alph Arabe	UGARIT	Alph. Latin	Alph Arabe
	A	أ		Y	ي		P (F)	ف
	B	ب		K	ك		ṣ =	ص
	G	ع		š =	ش		Q	ق
	ḥ =	غ		L	ل		R	ر
	D	د		M	م		t =	ث
	H	ه		d =	ذ		ǵ =	غ
	W	و		N	ن		T	ت
	Z	ز		ẓ =	ظ		I	إ
	ḥ =	ح		S	س		U	ؤ
	ṭ =	ط		' =	ع		(S)	(س)

decorated with lions, antelopes and hunters in exquisite relief work. There are gold necklaces and a silver statuette of a god with a gold kilt and a gold mallet raised as if to beat a gong. There are curiosities, too: a complete set of scale-weights, for example, beautifully carved in the form of kneeling cows, getting smaller and smaller until the last is a tiny miniature. The original tablet on which the Ugarit alphabet is inscribed is on exhibition at the Damascus Museum but at Aleppo one can gaze uncomprehendingly at tablets written in it, including a dictionary whose words are listed in ruled columns exactly as they are today. There is also a chart comparing the Ugarit alphabet with those that suceeded it – Aramaic, Hebrew, Latin and Arabic. What is remarkable is how different they are – how variously men of different cultures solved the same problems of encoding written speech.

BEEHIVES
AND BEDOUIN

ALEPPO IS the ideal centre for exploring Northern Syria. To the east lies the road to the Euphrates and its great new dam at El Thaura. South-west lies the site of ancient Ebla, at Tell Mardikh. To the west lies St Simeon's pillar surrounded by its great basilica at Qalaat Semaan. All these are described in other chapters of this book. Travelling in any of these directions, you will be impressed by the aridity of the countryside. It is not so much the Syrian desert, which lies further south-east, but the steppe of Syria. The north-south road from Aleppo to Homs is the limit of practical cultivation. East of the road, there is an average rainfall of only 200 millimetres a year. Outside Aleppo the trees stop for 150 kilometres until you reach the Euphrates. The land stretches away, flat, parched and infinitely empty except for endless telegraph poles pegged along the sides of the highway and scatterings of white or mud-coloured boxes which are the villages. Low hills seem to float above the horizon on mirage lakes, and lorries far ahead along the straight road seem to take off into the sky. Here and there a plume of yellow dust rises, completely obscuring both the ploughman and the plough which is stoically preparing it for a meagre crop. For though the land is baked to the colour of sand, you realize that there is grazing here of a sort. Though it looks like no more than bristly stubble on the face of the dry earth, it unbelievably supports the many herds of brown sheep and black goats that pick their way across

it, forever on the move. This is Bedouin country. You will pass the long low-slung tents of a Bedouin encampment, with lines of washing stretched between them, or see their fires and kerosene lamps shimmering at night like beacons in the wastes of nothingness. Sometimes they have stopped to do a few days' cotton-picking. The Bedouin are perhaps the last free, self-sufficient, untaxable people in the world, forever moving on, with their homes and possessions kept simple enough to be packed on the backs of camels and donkeys. And yet even they have compromised with mechanization. Often, beside their lines of black tents, made of goats' hair and strung on poles, is parked a beaten-up Dodge or Chevrolet truck on which they will pack their movables, even their camels. It is a strange sight, amid the lorries piled top-heavily with bulging bales of cotton, to see camels roped in pairs and standing patiently on the back of a swaying truck as their owner moves them on from one desert area to another. That is not a romantic sight, but a real camel train is. The farther east, the more likely you are to see these long convoys of camels, often a hundred beasts strong, wending their wavy course among the distant scrub or dunes. Then they really do look like ships of the desert. The Bedouin will be shawled and wrapped, usually in black, against the wind and sun, and the weather-beaten faces of the women are blotched with the blue decorative markings, like tattooing, that they find attractive. I met one leading his flock by calling out to them – you can't discipline a camel, only persuade it – seated on a beautiful camel as white as milk, with his tiny son sprawled face downward over the front of his saddle.

Equally striking sights of this desolate countryside are the 'beehive' villages which still exist, though it looks as though their days are numbered. The word 'beehive' is a misnomer now that bees are kept in square hives. These clusters of conical mud roofs, joined together like honeycomb cells, look like nothing so much as an irregular arrangement of modern fibre egg-trays, up-ended, with much the same grainy texture. There are several built off the roads leading out of Aleppo and to visit one is to step into a kind of peasant life that has not changed for centuries. The whole village is built of sun-dried mud and surrounded by attractively contoured mud walls that glow a golden biscuit-colour in the evening light. Inside the wall, other mud partitions criss-cross the village making enclosures and courtyards, each with its cluster of egg-domes. In Arabic they are called *Beyt Kobbi* – 'heap houses'. Their construction is simple, do-it-yourself and perfectly adapted to the terrain and local materials. The conical walls are two feet thick to keep the house cool by day and warm by night – they say the temperature inside does not vary. Each cone is about ten feet across at the base and is laid in courses of mud brick, mixed with straw on the inside surface, but left perfectly smooth outside to deflect heat (or rain, in that unlikely event). So smooth, indeed, that a series of small stone spikes are left sticking out of the side and at the apex to enable a man to climb up them to do repairs. There is one low door-way and one small window-hole near the top for ventilation and inside there is just about room to swing a cat. Hence the clusters: one beehive is used to live in, another to sleep in, another for cooking and wash-

ing. As the family grows, you can always add another cell. They are kept very clean, sparsely but attractively furnished with mats and a big painted chest to hold everything. Each home is a secret, private place walled into its courtyard, with its vine and its few head of cattle and poultry. But it is sad to see, all too often, that the beehive pattern is being more and more broken by little flat

Beehive houses of mud, clustered together like upturned egg-trays, keep cool by day and warm by night

topped (and surely much hotter) houses, whose attraction is that they show that you are rich enough to build one. So, on the edges of the villages, beehives are being abandoned and allowed to fall into ruin, or kept only as out-houses for poultry, donkeys and animal feed. Keeping up with the Joneses is a universal weakness, but one doubts whether the Joneses, in their ugly little white boxes, are really better off. All too soon, the beehive village will be only a memory, unless some are preserved as a tourist attraction.

There is one direction out of Aleppo which leads, not to arid land, but south-west to the most fertile part of Syria, the valley of the river Orontes. For centuries the Orontes drained away into unhealthy

The telephone lines lead on towards the coastal mountain range

Family laundry in the Orontes

marshland. Its transformation by draining and irrigation into the most fertile area of Syria is one of the achievements of planning in the republic since 1970. The plain, running north to south between the coastal mountains and the highlands along the road to Aleppo, is called the Ghab. Where once, they say, Egyptian pharoahs hunted elephant in the marshes, there now lies a huge chequerboard of green and golden crops growing in the red earth, outlined in rectangles by canals. The earth is refreshingly green (it seems remarkable to see cows and grass!) and on the higher slopes of the valley around Idlib, it blossoms in spring with millions of fruit trees and olives. The orchards are loaded with cherries, plums and pomegranates. The most interesting place from which to see the Ghab spread out beneath you is Qalaat al-Mudiq, where an

Arab fortress sits on top of a commanding hill, above an ancient caravanserai. The other side of the hill hides a large, forgotten Graeco-Roman city, the city of Apamea. The combination of these with the pleasures of travelling through fertile country makes an excursion to Qalaat al-Mudiq well worthwhile. Beneath the castle hill, on the main north-south valley road, stands a *khan*, or caravanserai, that has been preserved exactly as it was in Ottoman times. A pointed entrance arch leads into a vast, flagged courtyard, surrounded by round arched stables, with a drinking trough like a swimming pool in the middle. It is a forgotten but evocative place, a Hilton by the standards of its time, where it is easy to imagine the bustle of caravans getting ready to depart. Underneath the arches in one corner four pieces of a huge mosaic pavement

Family laundry

have been mounted on the stable wall like a jigsaw puzzle, aching to be put together. They show the wild animals that used to range the region, including a lion tackling what appears to be a wart-hog. If so, it is a piece of accurate observation. In Africa, where they are nowadays found, wart-hogs are known to be more than a match for lion unless the lion attacks the wart-hog from behind, which is exactly what this lion is doing. The pavement, of course, comes from nearby Apamea. The castle itself, perched on its hill, still shelters inhabitants in the ramshackle houses within its fortifications. The crusaders held it in the name of the Prince of Antioch until they lost it to the Arabs in 1149. Earthquakes damaged it even more. It does not compare with other Syrian castles, but it offers a spectacular view from the ramparts over the wide and lush Orontes valley.

Apamea, which lies concealed in the hillside away from the valley, is another matter. Here stands the half-excavated wreckage of what was a great city in Antony and Cleopatra's time, a city of more than 100,000 inhabitants with nearly five miles of city walls. It was established around 300 BC by Alexander the Great's successor, Seleucus, who named it after his wife, Apamea. It was a depot for training war elephants and breeding war horses, and was the second city of Hellenistic Syria. Cleopatra stayed here when visiting Antony, who was campaigning on the Euphrates. About AD 50 it became a Roman metropolis, visited by Roman emperors. Yet for centuries it disappeared entirely. The ruins were found buried under the hillside in 1930 but even the regular excavations of the last fourteen years have only scraped out a scene of impressive chaos. Apamea was brought down in ruins by two earthquakes in 1157 and 1170 and, looking at it today, one would believe they had only just occurred. The site

looks like the playground of a giant Roman child who had been playing with building blocks and kicked them over in a temper. The ground is shoulder-deep in a litter of great blocks and lumps of cut stone. You scramble over them, lying where they fell, to reach the main street of the city – called the Decumanus – which was lined with immense columns on either side. Sections of the colonnade have been re-erected and stand there, battered but magnificent, with their spiral fluting, their Corinthian capitals and chunks of the frieze and entablature they supported, catching the light and throwing sharp shadows on the golden stone. You can edge and scramble along this proud main thoroughfare, erected in the second century AD, admiring the architectural grace that it combined with such massiveness. It ran dead straight for more than a mile: nobody knows exactly how long, for both ends of the paved street are still lost in rubble. The sight of a line of nineteen columns, their fluting twisted like barley sugar, is impressive enough to make one wonder at the thought of the complete perspective. The shops lay under the colonnades on either side. You can still see the raised pavements where they have been dug out and it was here that the mosaics were found which are now in museums at Damascus, Hamah and Brussels – for Belgian archaeologists have done the excavating. A very large theatre has been found, though it is a shattered mess of remnants of the seating and stage wall. There are the foundations of a temple, a forum, public baths and a palace. There are also traces of Christian churches – for the city continued to be an important Christian centre long after the Romans left. It is hard to believe that a city which boasted 600 elephants among its population has sunk from sight as completely as this. Now all are gone, elephants, Romans, Christians and visiting emperors. The columns stand

The twisted columns of Apamea, once the second city of Syria mutely witnessing to Apamea's former glory. More of them lie jumbled in cylindrical sections on the ground.

Travelling between Aleppo and Damascus you are bound to pass through Hamah and Homs. Homs is a place to miss: Hamah is a place to stop! Hamah is famous for water-wheels, the biggest and most ancient in the world which are still working, but that is not all there is to see. It is an historic town, once ruled by its own kings, who fought off the Assyrians in 850 BC. Its situation beside the Orontes makes it one of the most tranquil and attractive small cities in Syria. The best way to approach it is across the narrow old stone bridge over the river, ending in a pointed archway set in the very walls of the old houses that rise sheer above the water. The walls are charmingly encumbered with antique and sagging balconies of sun-blistered wood, buttressed on carved wooden struts projecting over the river. They look like little shuttered summer houses hanging in the air and are reflected, like the domes above them, in the rippling blue water. But the sound you hear is not the running of the river but the mournful music of the huge water-wheel, or *noria*, that endlessly revolves close up against the houses, spilling spray and grinding in an eternal circle, driven by the river itself. It is an extraordinary sound that is made by these extraordinary objects, which have been called 'poems come to life'. The *noria* creaks, it moans, it splashes and it smacks as each of its projecting wooden teeth hits the water. At times it sounds like the putt-putt of a grumpy motor-mower, complaining on a steep bank of grass. With time, it becomes almost restful. At least one presumes so, because just above it one of the houses is equipped with a delightful, blue-tiled verandah for sitting out. The sound of the *noria* just below must be loud indeed, and unceasing day and night. The purpose of these

The Roman road that ran into Northern Syria from Turkey, alongside its modern replacement

giant wheels was, and is, to scoop up river water at the bottom and spill it out at the top into channels that feed the luxuriant gardens and orchards. There are some ten *norias* scattered up and down the river, most of them still working. One of them, which supplies the Great Mosque, dates from the fourteenth century. All the others are at least 300 years old. But the *noria* was invented on the Orontes long before that for it is depicted in one of the fourth-century mosaic pavements found at Apamea and now in the Damascus National Museum. You can examine its construction more easily further along the river but it would be a mistake to

113

The teenage ploughboy

The girl shepherd with her flock

leave this inviting, paintable bridge without crossing it. The old houses on the farther side have seen better days. Through one of the shuttered windows level with the bridge, a grey horse looks out, nibbling. You plunge under the arch at the end of the bridge through walls at least ten feet thick into caverns of gloom, arches upon arches, vault upon vault, tunnelled underneath the houses like the crypt of a church. The pas-sageway twists and turns between serried stone blocks with catacombs opening on either side, lighted – or rather left in gloom – by the occasional naked bulb. The passages lead out tortuously into a climbing street where outdoor staircases lead up to richly carved and panelled doors. Three-wheeled vehicles clatter through the arch-ways. From one disappearing passageway comes the insistent cry of a child, from

114

another snatches of an Arab song. Life is being lived secretly and invisibly somewhere above the twisting lanes of this river-encircled citadel. The women you see are fully veiled, showing not a chink of their faces. Hamah is known for the strictness of its Muslim observance, and for its old-fashioned, almost feudal ways. Until the 1963 revolution, labourers worked the land for the landowners without wages: they were fed and looked after but were virtually feudal serfs. There have been rich and aristo-cratic Syrian families in Hamah for genera-tions and there still are: their gardens front the Orontes and their houses are concealed in the trees.

You can visit Hamah's own Azem Palace, built by and named after the same Pasha el-Azem as the Azem Palace in Damascus. He was governor of both places in the early

The road winds down to the fertile Orontes valley

Ploughing the hard way on the stony plateau

Ships of the desert in convoy

Cotton growers: the weighing of the crop

Cotton growers

eighteenth century. It has a dazzlingly opulent, decorated interior under a red dome
and is luxuriantly set in gardens and courtyards. It is now a museum of Islamic art.
And you should not leave Hamah without
walking alongside the Orontes, upstream to
where a pleasant restaurant borders the
river, entitled the Casino of the Four Norias.
You can walk down the river bank to inspect
these at close quarters. One is almost as big
as a fairground's Big Wheel and yet it is
turned effortlessly by the river. Here you
can see clearly how it operates. Around the
rim of the wheel project a set of spade-
shaped teeth which are caught by the water.
Attached to them is a set of what look like
wooden shoe-boxes, or rabbit hutches,
which scoop up the water and spill it out at
the top of each revolution into an aqueduct.
They not only spill the water out at the top

but all the way up, for they leak prodi-
giously, losing half of what they scoop. It
is an absurdly inefficient way of transporting
water – but it is time-honoured and it is
free. The hubs of the wheels are made of fat
sections of tree-trunk revolving in wooden
sockets. They are heavily greased but one
wonders how long it takes before the axle
wears away. Ponderously, grotesquely, they
turn and churn, outlasting generations of
human life. Little boys jump in the river to
use them as breathtaking rides in an ancient
amusement park. They catch hold of one of
the projections as the wheel comes through
the water and ride with it, up, up and right
over the top, where they jump from fifty
feet into the river below. It is a symbolic
sight. The wheel tosses off its human cargo
and churns on, creaking away like time
itself, unable to stop.

Statue of a richly-robed goddess, Palmyra Museum

PALMYRA

PERHAPS THE finest sonnet Shelley wrote describes how he met 'a traveller from an antique land' who told him of a great statue lying shattered in the desert, with this proud inscription on its pedestal:

'My name is Ozymandias, king of kings:
　Look on my works, ye Mighty, and
　　　　despair!
Nothing beside remains. Round the decay
Of that colossal wreck, boundless and bare
The lone and level sands stretch far away.'

There could be no better epitaph for Palmyra, the legendary city of the Syrian desert. If Shelley's lines on the futility of human vainglory have ever moved you, you will experience that emotion, and that awe, more vividly at Palmyra than anywhere else in the Near East. Even by the shortest route from Homs, you have to cross 100 miles of desert to reach it. By the direct route from Damascus it is 200 miles. And after you have traversed waste upon waste of solitude along the old caravan route from coastal Syria towards Mesopotamia and the Arabian Gulf, patrolled only by vultures and the grazing camels of the Bedouin, comes the surprise that cannot fail to make you catch your breath and feel at one with explorers of past ages. Desert hills rise gently out of the flat sand. The track winds between them, rounds a bend, and there, suddenly, below you lies an oasis, a great dark pool of palm trees in vivid green. Beside it stretch the ruins of a fabulous, classical city, columns of columns marching across the desert like an imperial army. It stands silent and golden and all around, 'boundless and bare, The lone and level sands stretch far away'.

It is the sheer size of it – six square kilometres – that first takes the breath away: then, as you descend into it, the beauty, even in decay, of 'that colossal wreck'. Roman as it looks first, it is not the grandeur of Rome that you are looking at. It is an Arab grandeur. It was the most extraordinary civilization that the Arabs produced in the first three centuries after Christ: Palmyra, a kingdom in its own right, built by Palmyrenes out of their own wealth and importance, earned from their position at the halfway point of all the caravan routes across the Syrian desert, which met there like the spokes of a wheel converging at the hub.

When the caravans ceased, so did Palmyra. It has all the mystery of a lost city – for it literally was lost for centuries, unknown to the civilized world, which by then had no need of it. When it was rediscovered in 1751 by two English travellers, who brought back their reports and drawings and published them in a book, the world gasped. It was like the discovery of the Incas. Suddenly, there was a new civilization of which nobody knew, not merely a ruined city but the centre of an empire which ruled from Egypt to Asia Minor for a few proud reckless years, then crashed just as swiftly from its pinnacle into ruin and oblivion. What a romantic fall was there – for its empire was achieved and lost under a woman, perhaps the most remarkable woman of the ancient world, Queen Zenobia. She was the widow of the king who first raised Palmyra to proud independence, Odenathus. We do not know whom Shelley was thinking of when he coined the name Ozymandias, but he would have been familiar, as a Romantic, with the still-fresh story of Palmyra. He could, with perfect truth, have written 'My name is Odenathus, king of kings' for that is exactly the inscription and the title which Odenathus put on one of the statues of himself. King of kings – like Shah-an-Shah in Persia – was the traditional title for the emperor of a Semitic empire, and this great general had done what the Romans could not do. He had defeated the Persians and driven them out of Syria, which he proceeded to annex from Rome as his own.

It is possible to see Palmyra on a day's visit – you can also go by air – but it is a waste of one of life's great visual experiences. That is to see the sun set and the sun rise over this amazing monument to a vanished people. Dawn is perhaps the most dramatic spectacle. At five o'clock the site is a chilling wilderness of fantastic, looming shadows. The stars are almost incredibly near, bright and sharp in the crisp desert air, swept by a cutting southerly wind. The place to stand is near the Great Colonnade, the central avenue of the city, thirty-five feet wide, which is still lined by dozens of the thirty-foot Corinthian pillars that stretched along both sides for nearly a mile, connecting the two major temples of the city. Inch by inch the sun lifts its rim into view above the still-black smudge of the palm grove. It comes up, not fiery red, but brazen yellow between the columns, picking them out like rows of sentinels from the shadows. First of all the outer acanthus leaves of their Corinthian capitals are tipped with light, then the outlines of the pillars themselves, like an

Going to work just after dawn in Palmyra

ordered grove of sturdy trees. Gradually the colour floods into the stone to produce the glow of Palmyra – an effect of light on desert-swept stone which cannot be completely captured in paint, in colour photography or in words. It isn't quite golden. It isn't quite rose-pink. It isn't quite amber or alabaster or topaz. It is a vibrancy, a coming-and-going of light and reflection and colour

harmonies that produce an almost visible quivering that cannot be analysed. It is almost supernatural. It is almost as if the shapes were made, not of hard stone, but of water At one end of the long perspective, the light picks out the square-shouldered block of the Temple of Bel, the chief deity of Palmyra. At the end of the avenue leading to the temple, it gilds the delicate arc of the triumphal arch whose carved supporting panels of leaves, rosettes and flowers are still chisel-edged in stone. It comes to the theatre lying beside the avenue, and fills the snug, intimate semi-circle of its auditorium with bouncing light and warmth, as though the spotlights had just come on for a perform-ance for which those horse-shoe benches are waiting to fill with people. A third of the

A funeral bust of a grandee, in the Palmyra Museum

Palmyra: the elegant portico of the Funerary Temple at one end of the Great Colonnade

way along the avenue it comes to the cross-roads, the city centre. This is marked by the tetrapylon, four groups of four columns, each raised on a stone platform, each supporting an entablature like a small table-top. The whole group was designed to show off four statues and look from a distance like a piece of highly decorated antique furniture. Beside the tetrapylon lies the *agora*, or colonnaded market square, where the Palmyrenes held their public assemblies; adjoining that, the little Senate House, from which the city was ruled. Looking far, far down to the other end of the avenue, the vista is closed by the portico of the elegant funerary temple, a portico leading now to nothing but air

and a great jumble of fallen masonry on the ground. Beyond all, perched theatrically in the air on a steep desert hillside, stands the romantic Arab castle, which was built long after the city fell into ruin but which contrasts picturesquely with the classical order and regularity of the streets and monuments below. The light by now has bathed the conical and concave slopes of the desert hills, rugged and strangely contoured by the wind and now warmed to a purplish red. The dogs begin to bark. Desert crows plane over the heads of the pillars in creaking pairs, against a sky which has now turned vivid blue. Donkey carts are beginning to rumble and squeak down the dusty roads to

Palmyra: looking through the Great Colonnade with its empty brackets for statues

work – on the restorations and on the building of the new hotel. The heat begins to hum in the sand. Little dusty desert birds begin to prink and peep, hidden among the great blocks of fallen stone. The sun is well up over the Temple of Bel. Palmyra is beginning another day of empty grandeur, trooping its columns like guardsmen, watched by the irregular hills and hummocks of the eternal desert landscape that becalms it like an island in an ocean of sand and solitude. It is time for breakfast – and for a little history to bring this amazing necropolis to imaginative life.

Palmyra was originally – and now is again – known by its Arab name of Tadmor and owes its existence to a spring, the Efqa spring, which gushes out beside the palm groves from an underground water-course of slightly sulphurous water. It has been fed through canals to water the date-palms, from which the town gets its name. There is also a sweet-water spring a few miles to the north-west which supplied the town with drinking water through an aqueduct built in Roman times. This lucky accident of nature has made Tadmor an inhabited place since the Stone and Bronze ages. It is mentioned in the Mari tablets of 1800 BC and referred to in the Old Testament. But it was not until the coming of the caravan trade with Eastern Asia that it grew wealthy. After the introduction of camels from Bactria, in perhaps about 1000 BC, it was practicable to cross the Syrian desert by the shortest route, across the middle. This was the beginning of the 'Silk Route' bringing goods from China and India, via the Arabian Gulf and Mesopotamia to the Mediterranean Coast of Phoenicia (now Lebanon) and thus to Europe. Right where it was most needed, at the halfway point, stood Tadmor with its water supply – for which visitors were charged – providing a secure stopping place protected against raiding nomads.

Gradually the oasis settlement grew into a city that provided more and more services to the traders. It had its own camel corps, which caravans hired for their protection and guidance across the desert. It provided not only provisions on the long trek but finance and marketing. Before long it must have made sense for caravans coming from East and West to meet there, exchange goods and go back the way they came, thus halving their journeys. So into Palmyra came the riches of the East – silk and jade from China, perfumes, spices and jewels, ebony and ivory from India, carpets and glassware, olive oil, nuts and figs, wine and cheese, all of them subject to tax in transit. In AD 137 a great stone tablet, fifteen feet wide, was inscribed with the 'Tariff of Palmyra', setting out the regulations and charges for each commodity decreed by the senate, including the fees payable for supplying water. By then Palmyra's merchants had their own trading empires – one carving shows a merchant standing proudly beside his merchant ship, which no doubt sailed the Arabian Gulf. There are records of Palmyrene traders established in the Gulf, in the cities of the Tigris, of Egypt and even in Europe. Palmyra became the Venice of the Near East, a Venice in a sea of sand, her ships the convoys of camels that went out from her gates. Her chief rival in trade was Petra on the southern caravan route but in

AD 105 Petra and its kingdom was reduced to an appendage of the Roman empire. After that Palmyra reigned alone. Its population reached perhaps 200,000. The Romans left Palmyra alone as an almost independent state on the borders of their province of Syria, which was founded by Pompey in 64 BC. Once again geography came to its aid. Rather than subjugate and garrison it with legions, far out in the desert, the Romans saw the convenience of allowing it to remain autonomous. Palmyra supplied its own army of mounted archers and became a buffer state protecting the eastern fringe of the empire in the no-man's-land between the Romans and the raiding Parthians from the Persian empire. It was in both sides' interest to let trade with the East continue. Palmyra was tacitly left in peace to prosper. The Emperor Hadrian declared it a free city in AD 129, and in 212 Septimus Severus, an emperor with a Syrian wife and Syrian sympathies, gave it the status of a Roman *colonia*, or colony, which meant that its citizens had equal rights with those of Rome and were free of taxes. The city was then governed by its own senate, which was dominated by the leading merchant families. Walking along the Great Colonnade, you look up at stone projections, or consoles, mounted on each of the pillars, overhanging the street. They were the brackets on which statues were mounted of the merchants and benefactors who were honoured by the city – perhaps because they helped pay to have the pillars built. The inscriptions tell of their achievements, often those of being a successful businessman. One caravan tycoon of AD 160 was honoured by having ten such monuments to his name. Curiously enough, very few public statues have survived from the great days of Palmyra – tomb effigies are another subject which we shall come to later – and it has been suggested that they may have been of bronze and were later melted down by pillagers. At all events, this intensely businesslike and wealthy community of middlemen – like the City of London – built itself the richest and most luxurious city of the region, beautified no doubt with the services of Greek and Roman architects. Gradually it passed from being a republic, governed by a wealthy oligarchy, into a kingdom. The family of Odenathus proclaimed themselves princes of Palmyra, and ruled the city from AD 235 to 272. In 260 the Persians invaded the Eastern provinces of the Roman empire, defeated the legions and captured the Emperor Valerian. At this moment Palmyra's prince, Odenathus the Younger, rescued Rome. A great general, he twice defeated the Persian armies under their emperor Shahpur, pursued them to the gates of their capital Ctesiphon (near modern Baghdad) and was given the title 'Augustus' and 'Corrector of the Orient' by a grateful Rome. He behaved like a Roman emperor himself. But in 267 he and his eldest son were mysteriously murdered at Homs. His second wife, Zenobia, became queen regent on behalf of her son, Wahb-Allat, who was under age. With Zenobia came the last, brief heyday of Palmyra, which was to last a mere five years. Zenobia was comparable in fame to Cleopatra, from whom she claimed to be descended, but of far greater ability. She was as hardy as any man, hunted game and could march for miles at the head of her troops, but she was not just an Amazon. She spoke four languages – Aramaic (the language of Palmyra), Egyptian, Greek and Latin, and read Homer and Plato. She employed, as her tutor and adviser, the philosopher Longinus, the chief Syrian intellectual of his time. Gibbon describes her person in his *The Decline and Fall of the Roman Empire* in glowing terms: 'She equalled in beauty her ancestor Cleopatra and far surpassed that princess in chastity and valour.

Zenobia was esteemed the most lovely as well as the most heroic of her sex. She was of dark complexion. Her teeth were of a pearly whiteness and her large black eyes sparkled with an uncommon fire, tempered by the most attractive sweetness. Her voice was strong and harmonious. Her manly understanding was strengthened and adorned by study.'

She also had a sense of humour. The story has come down of how she punished a merchant for overcharging. The man was sent for to appear at the theatre, where the queen and the audience awaited him to witness his punishment. The wretched man stood quivering with fear, expecting a wild beast to be loosed upon him. When the animal was brought in there was a roar of laughter. He looked round – and saw it was a cock.

Zenobia called herself 'The Queen of the East' and soon proceeded to justify it by leading her troops to conquer the whole of Roman Syria, part of Asia Minor and into Egypt as far as Alexandria, which she captured in 270. There her pride led to her undoing. Not only did she declare full independence from Rome, she ordered coins to be minted in Alexandria which bore her head, or that of her son, with the title 'Augusta' and 'Augustus' respectively. This was too much independence for Rome to stomach. She had reckoned without the capable new emperor, Aurelian, a fine cavalry commander who was restoring Rome's faltering grip over its empire. He decided Zenobia had to be stopped, marched an army to Syria and twice defeated her and her forces, at Antioch and at Homs, in 271. She had to retreat to Palmyra itself, where he besieged her. He cut off the route to Persia, from which she hoped to get support, and offered her generous surrender terms. Zenobia imperiously refused them. Recklessly, she decided to make a dash for Persia in person to appeal for military aid.

Palmyran tomb-carving: a richly-dressed merchant, with cup, surrounded by his family

She crossed the encircling Roman lines on a dromedary and reached the Euphrates. The Roman cavalry caught up with her and captured her as she was stepping into a boat to cross the river. Hearing their queen was a captive, the Palmyrenes opened the gates of their city to the Romans. Aurelian proved a generous victor by the standards of the time – at first. The city was fined for its rebellion. Some of the prominent citizens were deported and Zenobia's adviser, Longinus, was executed, for all his fame as an author (his *Treatise on the Sublime* is still studied by scholars). Zenobia herself was taken to Rome as Aurelian's chief trophy, the captive Queen of the East. Accounts of Aurelian's triumph in 274 in the capital describe how lions, elephants and a thousand gladiators took part in the procession. Zenobia herself had to follow the emperor's chariot in chains – but they were chains made of gold. Aurelian himself respected her as a redoubtable enemy. He wrote in a letter: 'Those who say I have only conquered a woman do not know what that woman was, nor how lightning were her decisions, how persevering she was in her plans, how resolute with her soldiers.' Zenobia's last days are clouded by contradictory legends. One story is that Aurelian offered to marry her but she refused him. Another, that she retired to comfortable captivity in a villa at Tivoli with her small son. Another, that she married a Roman nobleman and raised

129

another family. Another, that she fasted to death rather than live on in captivity. You can choose which ending you prefer to the life of this outstanding queen. The ending of the great age of her city came with brutal suddenness in the previous year, 273. Palmyra rose in revolt against its Roman overlords, massacred the garrison of 600 archers and the Roman governor and sent an invitation to Zenobia to return. Aurelian sent his legions back to put down the rising and this time, under their general Bassus, they showed no mercy. Men, women and children were massacred, the city plundered and set on fire. Aurelian, hearing of this, sent orders to stop the killing and provided money to make good the damage to the Temple of Bel. But Palmyra never recovered from this catastrophic defeat. The days of independence were over. Henceforward it was a Roman frontier town. Diocletian, emperor from 284 to 305, turned it into an armed camp as a strong-hold in the line of fortresses across the desert that marked the boundary of the empire. What is called 'Diocletian's Camp', lying to the north-west at the far end of the Great Colonnade, is still being excavated. It is believed to have been built on the site of Zenobia's palace, of which there is no trace. In the sixth century, Justinian rebuilt the city's defence walls. But by this period the population and its economy was dwindling along with the desert caravan route. In 634, the armies of Islam occupied Palmyra with scarcely a fight and the Temple of Bel was converted into an Arab fortress. In the tenth century a severe earthquake finished off the destruction of the city, along with that of Baalbek. Most of the columns and public buildings fell and for centuries afterwards the desert winds buried most of the ruins in sand drifts of up to twenty feet deep. Palmyra virtually disappeared. All that remained was the fortified Temple of Bel, inside whose walls a small

Palmyran carving

Arab village – once more called Tadmor – survived as best it could against raiding Bedouin.

Two English merchants living in Aleppo, who had heard tales of the city buried in the desert, went on an expedition to look for it in 1678. They were held captive by the local Bedouin who demanded ransom but, seemingly undeterred by this, they paid a later visit with a pastor called Halifax, who copied some of the inscriptions he found on the stones of the Temple of Bel. A record of this visit inspired an English antiquary called Robert Wood, seventy years later, to go in search of the lost city. In 1751 he reached it

with a friend called Dawkins. They made detailed architectural drawings and copies of the inscriptions in Palmyrene script – a twenty-two letter alphabet, written from right to left. In 1753, Robert Wood published his description and his drawings in a book which astonished his contemporaries – *The Ruins of Palmyra* – which is now a highly-prized rarity. It was, wrote Wood, 'the greatest quantity of ruins we had ever seen and beyond them a flat waste as far as the eye could reach . . . a most romantic variety of prospect'. By then the Palmyrene script had been deciphered and recognized as a form of Aramaic and the story of Oden-

athus and Zenobia's rise and fall seized the imagination of European readers. Above all, they were fascinated by the fact that nobody had known it was there. Neither, indeed, did anyone know of the existence of Petra, ('the rose-red city half as old as time'), whose ruins, carved out of the Jordanian mountains, were not discovered until the early nineteenth century. In 1817, Robert Wood's book on Palmyra was republished – the very year Shelley wrote his sonnet on Ozymandias, king of kings – at the height of the Romantic Movement's fascination with the Near East.

A few years before that, one of the great

131

English eccentrics, Lady Hester Stanhope, who had run away from England to marry a desert sheikh, rode into Palmyra in Bedouin dress to be given a Bedouin welcome. Along the Great Colonnade the brackets on the pillars were occupied by Arab dancing girls. One of them was lowered by rope from the triumphal arch to place a crown on her head, conferring on her the Freedom of the Desert. It was like a scene out of a film epic by Cecil B. de Mille. Lady Hester pitched camp in the temple precincts and stayed for a week. After that, the ruins were fairly often visited by hardy and curious travellers. Even in 1912 Baedeker advised the necessity of an armed escort to make the nine-day expedition, out and back, from Damascus.

Excavations did not begin until 1924 and, under pre-war French rule, the Arab village was moved out of the Temple of Bel to the site where the town of Tadmor stands now, apart from the ruins. Many archaeologists of many nationalities have worked there since and movable carvings, especially from the graves, have found their way into museums abroad, in Copenhagen, the Louvre and elsewhere. Restoration has gone on steadily. In 1950 there were 150 columns standing. Now there are more than 300 and about fiften more are re-erected every year. Some of the earlier restorations are, on close inspection, rather crassly done. The columns of the tetrapylon, for example, all except for one original, are of poured cement mixture too smooth to be convincing, though there is a weighty excuse – each group of columns carries 150 tons of cornice. Dr Khaled Assad, the Director of Antiquities, assured me that the policy of cement patching has now been stopped. Steel bars are inserted to hold together the original fragments of the stone jig-saw puzzle unaltered. It is easy to distinguish the newly-restored blocks in structures like the triumphal arch, for exam-

ple. Buried in sand, they remained as ivory white as they were originally. The stone that remained standing is gently bronzed by time and weather. The columns which survived standing are eaten away to a short distance above the base, by the scouring effect of the wind whipping up the desert sand to this height. Even now, only about a quarter of the vast site has been excavated. It is tempt-

Palmyra: the *agora*, or main square, with part of the Great Colonnade and the tetrapylon in the distance

ing to speculate what else of this remarkable metropolis still awaits discovery. Like a Marie Celeste of the desert, Palmyra would be amazing even if there were no traces left of the people who lived in it. But the ruins are not totally bereft of humanity. The Palmyrenes left behind images of themselves in their family tombs, which are as lively in their way as anything in ancient Egypt. Sur-rounding the city limits on the north and west is the city of the dead, or rather three distinct suburbs of the dead, each with its own type of tomb. One is a tomb built like a small temple decorated with columns, of which the grandest example is the funerary temple which closes one end of the Great Colonnade with its elegant portico. Another is the tower-tomb, a square structure like a little fort or watchtower, in which the dead were interred in the walls on landings reached by an internal staircase. One of the towers has five storeys and some are big enough to have held up to 400 bodies. They are the oldest buildings surviving in the city, dating from the first century AD. But the most fascinating of all are the underground galleries, called *hypogea*, as big as houses, hewn out of the rock in the Valley of the Tombs to the west of the city. The dead were buried in a series of shelved underground chambers decorated by busts and sculptured reliefs, depicting not only the dead man but his family as well. It was the custom for families to gather at the tomb for a funeral feast. Its centre-piece was the corpse who reclines on a couch on one elbow holding a cup and gazing serenely at us. The best preserved of these tombs, the *Hypogea of Jarhai*, dated AD 108 was transported en bloc to the Damascus Museum, where it forms a stunning, underground exhibit, like a salon filled with a party of silent, stone guests. On the site itself you can see similar family groups in the niche of one of the tower-tombs and in the underground 'Tomb of the Three Brothers', where painted portraits of the dead survive as murals surrounding the niches in which they were interred. But the best place to study these citizens of the golden age of the city is in the Palmyra Museum, which is a treasury of its social history. They are not, it must be said, a beautiful race. There sit, for example, the family Malqo or the family Bolberk in their 'eternal abode', as the inscriptions call the tombs, holding cups and looking for all the world as if this were an eternal tea-party at which news of aunts and cousins was being discussed, along with the price of silk or camels, and how well a young nephew was doing as an export agent in Italy or Spain. Allowances must be made, of course, for the fact that this is a funeral feast, part of the cult of the dead, and for the limitations of the sculptors who stuck rigidly to convention. But the impression is oddly domestic and cosy and yet solemn, like Victorians taking themselves seriously for a family photograph – in a word, bourgeois. Their faces are broad and full, with strong, straight noses, oriental almond-shaped eyes and narrow, down-turned, often almost cruel mouths. They look stern, proud, businesslike and, above all, rich. They have the wary look of self-made men and women who have made their pile and are not going to let anyone forget it – even in the next world. They are dressed both in the Roman and the Parthian, or Persian, fashion. Their flowing robes have richly embroidered hems, ornamental belts and clasps and, often, pantaloons beneath their long tunics. They are literally loaded with jewellery. The women drip with earrings under their draped head-dresses. There are rings on their fingers and great stones studding the necklaces that surround their thick necks. They were, however, famous for their beautiful ears. The Palmyrene priests wear cylindrical hats, like pastry cooks. You may see the riches of this bourgeois society in the trappings of a camel being led by camel-drivers, or the harness of a horse being ridden by a soldier, by the dress of a shipowner standing proudly in front of his ship, with a long, curved dhow-like sail. And, of course, in the wives, their hair beautifully done. their draperies strictly in place, their jewels ostentatiously large, their servants in attendance and their expression stern, competent and matronly. One still bears traces of her painted lipstick. These sculptured families, mostly of the third century AD, were already generations away from the tented life of the desert. They had every convenience of their time. They spoke Greek and, some of them, Latin, as well as Aramaic, and added Latin names to their

Opposite:
The great Euphrates Dam provides Syria with its
electricity and irrigation for a vast,
previously arid tract of land

own. They had a flourishing intellectual life – witness the presence of a philosopher such as Longinus. And in art they added to Greek and Roman classicism a love of exuberant decoration and detail which is not classical at all. The friezes and lintels of their buildings were rich with patterns of rosettes and bunches of grapes and geometrical leaf-patterns that Roman purists would have disapproved of.

Their religion was completely Eastern in origin. They worshipped nearly thirty gods in all, chief of them the great Semitic god Bel, whose temple was the city's most magnificent single monument. If the colonnade of its main portico looks now like a row of badly eroded chimneys, that is because their Corinthian capitals were originally made of costly gilded bronze acanthus leaves, which were stripped off by plunderers after Palmyra's fall. Bel was worshipped with the sacrifice of beasts – you can see the ramp up which they were led to the inner temple and the sacrificial altar. Besides Bel, (also known as Bol or Baal), there were the sun and the moon gods, Yahribol and Aglibol, and Baal-Shahmin, represented as an eagle in a carving in the museum, the ruler of heaven. The little Temple of Baal-Shahmin, which lies on its own, away from the Great Colonnade in front of the Zenobia Hotel, is one of the most beautiful and best-restored buildings among the ruins. Other members of the pantheon of gods included the Arab and Babylonian gods, Allat and Ishtar. There was a god of wisdom and writing called Nabo, whose temple has also been unearthed beside the Great Colonnade, and even a god of caravans, Sharo. Here, in the tomb carvings, are the people who took part in these religious ceremonies, who thronged the Great Colonnade's arcaded pavements and shops, who sat in the Senate and attended the theatre, who watched the caravans arrive and depart in the *agora* and went home to their mosaic floors and Persian carpets to count their money. What opportunists they were! Undeterred by the inconvenience of such vast wastes of desert all around them, they raised a mercantile city as great as any in the East. For a century they might well have said to themselves: 'Look on my works, ye mighty, and despair!' Then with the same over-confidence that betrayed the heroes of Greek tragedy, they over-reached themselves and brought retribution and ruin on their heads. A little way beyond the Corinthian columns lies the small town of Tadmor, a poor place, the most that the oasis itself can support. Piles of freshly-picked dates lie heaped along the verges of the main street. There are no carpets, no luxuries for sale. The local restaurant is a bare café with neon lighting and a juke-box. The people live off the date trade and the tourist trade and as labourers on the excavations and restorations.

But for that accident of history and geography, that is all there would ever have been . . . a desert settlement around an oasis. But, instead of Tadmor, there was Palmyra, one of the sights of the ancient world, where you can still step immediately and vividly back into the past and re-live it.

135

Druze women gossiping

Outside Aleppo, a Bedouin girl herds goats and sheep on the sparse stubble

Camel trains, flocks and beehive villages relieve the emptiness of the desert country that stretches for hundreds of kilometres beyond Aleppo

Sunrise at Palmyra

Palmyra's golden colonnade stretches away to the
Temple of Bel (below, left) beside the oasis that
brought it prosperity and brief independence

The people of Bosra live in the marvellously preserved ruins of a Roman provincial capital, with the finest theatre in the Near East, and walk the Roman streets among the arches, gates and fallen columns

ROMANS
AND DRUZES

THE FAR south of Syria has a very different character from any other region. At first sight it has a sinister air, for it is a high, volcanic plateau, almost a wilderness, and the rock which breaks out in ridges and conical hills is black. It would appeal to none but the lovers of lost and lonely places were it not for two unique curiosities: first, it has the best-preserved remains of Roman Syria; second, it is the adopted home of a strange, handsome and secretive people, the Druzes. Both are fascinating subjects to investigate. In practice, it is best visited as a day's excursion from Damascus, for there are as yet no hotels for the tourist.

As you drive south-east from Damascus you have to cover sixty miles of wild, though level, country, passing over a great plateau of burnt sienna, gradually turning blacker as the basalt rock begins to break the surface. It is a military landscape with military airfields ringed by anti-aircraft guns and slit trenches concealed among grazing sheep. The goats are the colour of burnt toast. Here and there beside the road you will see a reminder of the fighting that has been waged in the skies above this hard, rocky plain in the recent wars with Israel. The memorials to Syrian fighter-pilots who fought over their home ground are surmounted by silver models of their planes on pedestals recording the number of their aerial victories.

Gradually the road has been climbing and getting blacker with basalt until it resembles the rocky moorlands of the Pennines, only darker, criss-crossed by exactly the same kind of dry-stone walls and stunted, crooked thorn trees. The wonder is that many people get a living from this unpromising landscape, for the soil, where there is any, is rich and the rainfall is less meagre than in the flatter land further north. Somehow vines, pasture, cattle and fig trees survive. At last there appears a cluster of volcanic, sugar-loaf hills, the outposts of the Jebel el-Druze, 'the mountain of the Druzes', which has been renamed the Jebel el-Arab. The Druzes, a tough, mountain people, settled here in the early eighteenth century, building villages that cling to the bases of these extinct volcanoes. When they arrived, it had been uninhabited land since the retreat of the Byzantine empire a thousand years before. What they found were the ruins of the Roman towns and Byzantine churches that remained from the region's 500 years of importance and prosperity as the centre of the Roman province of Arabia. Such was the depopulation of the succeeding centuries that no one had bothered to pull them down to build anything else. The first town you come to is Shahba, nestling in a ring of cones, one of which is called the Hill of the Messiah – *Tell al-Masiya* – with a tomb on the top in honour of Jesus and a legend that he appeared here after the Resurrection. It is a bustling little market town of 7000 people. It held 56,000 in Roman times and the town lives in the ruins of the Roman city as if in an overcoat that is several sizes

Bosra: the grandeur that was Rome is now a perch for doves

too big. Its claim to fame was that the one wholly Arab emperor was born here – Philip the Arab. He was proclaimed emperor by his legions in AD 244 and during his five-year reign gave orders to rebuild his home town as a Roman city named Philippopolis. That is why you enter and leave it through Roman arches, which mark the gates into the city walls – there are four in all. You will find the broken-off stumps of the four pillars of a tetrapylon (like that at Palmyra) at the main crossroads, flanked by the bus-stop and piles of water-melons on the pavement. You are standing, not at the bus-stop, but in the forum. From there one of the two main Roman streets climbs a hill to the right. It has the original Roman surface, its paving blocks still tightly in place, leading

When Bosra was a Roman capital in AD 106, the same games were played on this very street

past the shops where one can see a sheep tethered to a ring in the pavement and a couple of calves tied to a tree. On one side of the street three and a half Corinthian columns still stand in a row, the remains of the colonnade which lined the street. There is just one thing about them which comes as a shock. Unlike all the Corinthian columns one sees elsewhere in the ancient world, these are deep black, carved out of the omnipresent basalt. Behind them, the base of what was a temple has been utilized as the pedestal for a rather grand private house for a local chief. Just opposite, by way of contrast, a weaver lives in a cave-like shop, working a handloom, with his wife winding the bobbins of red, white and black wool for him. They are turning out seat-runners

Bosra's Roman high street, and the Gate of the Winds: the past and the future

in traditional patterns. Behind the loom, in the back of the cave, is where they live, working long hours to support a family of eight sons and a daughter. Climbing further up to the top of the hill one arrives at the 'Philippeion' – a square family tomb which the emperor Philip erected in honour of his father. Perhaps it was to win him a little posthumous respectability, for the old man was a notorious brigand. Until a few years ago it was used as the local school but now it has been cleared out and returned to its plain and severe original state. Also cleared and restored by the Department of Antiquities is the theatre behind it. It once seated 1700 spectators – not large by Roman standards, but still a theatre, in a place far out on the fringe of the touring circuit. Back down the hill and along from the forum-crossroads one finds excavations going on amid the massive foundations and arches of the baths. Just behind them, in a courtyard off a little side-street, women sit barefoot under an awning weaving twenty-foot long Bedouin carpets, taking it in turns to sit at the loom or to stand in the shade of the doorway watching and chatting, with their white muslin head-dresses falling down their backs. It is a cheerful, domestic court-yard with chickens and turkeys waddling about and a cow with swollen udders tucking into a bag of feed in the corner. Yet the stone-flagged floor and parapet is swept spotless, as in a Dutch painting. To sit down and watch, all you need do is to perch on one of the convenient rows of cylindrical stones that stand outside their dwelling. There seems to be something familiar about the shape . . . of course, these are sections of a Roman column. You are sitting, and they are living and weaving, in part of the ruins of the Roman baths! It is the sort of shock one comes to accept as normal in the Jebel el-Druze. Opposite, across the little side-street, stands a small but fascinating

museum. Once it was the site of a Roman villa of the grandest kind; indeed the museum was built to protect the ravishing set of six mosaics that were found intact there by the museum director, Hayel Amer, in 1961. There, still glowing with subdued colour, are Dionysos, Orpheus with his lyre, Mars, Venus being born from the sea, and the graceful, well-endowed ladies representing the four seasons, with a drunken Hercules admiring them in so far as he is capable. They are exquisite mosaics and, what is more, they are whole. Each of them is inscribed with the name of its subject in Greek characters – for the eastern Roman empire commonly spoke Greek, not Latin, except on official business. Mr Amer has done great things to preserve ancient Shahba. He found the pavements, directs the excavations, rescued the ruins from their former neglect and is a mine of information about the town. He also learned the art of mosaic himself and presented President Assad with his own very life-like portrait in the ancient technique.

The people in the streets of Shahba and the nearby hill towns immediately strike one as being different from those of any other part of Syria. They are different in dress, bearing, physique. They are Druzes. Their carriage is proud, their dress is opulent and colourful, their eyes are blue, their beauty and nobility is often striking. The women walk about unveiled with full skirts and tight waists, their dresses embroidered in glittering thread of gold or crimson or magenta under flowing head-dresses pulled back like the wimples of the fourteenth century. The men wear black cloaks and white *keffiyehs* and the elders of the sect wear white, bulbous turbans. They do not look like other Syrians. There has been much speculation about their origins – their blue eyes and the frequency of fair hair for long made travellers believe that they must have

The only tenant of one of Bosra's Roman ruins

Time passes in Bosra now the caravans have moved on

European ancestry from the invading soldiers of Alexander the Great or from the crusaders. This was imagination. Some scholars believe they are of mixed Mesopotamian and Persian origin, from where they migrated to Lebanon. At all events, they migrated to the Jebel el-Druze from the Lebanon mountains, near Baalbek. This was where the Druze religion was founded in the early years of the eleventh century and where there are still many Druzes in the mountain villages. Their religion is a closely-kept secret and it takes half a lifetime to be initiated into its mysteries. Their meeting houses are plain and unadorned and no one but a Druze believer may enter them. It is said that to be fully initiated a man must be fifty. After long preparation he is admitted as an elder, an *aqel* or 'enlightened one', privy to all the secrets of their sacred books, and must wear the white turban and black woollen robe. He must abstain from drinking, smoking, swearing and the company of women and must not cut his beard. I was received by the chief elder at Shahba, a man of eighty, bent and deaf and learned, who lived a most restricted life, only leaving his house to go to the Druze temple hidden away in a side-street. He had never married nor, I was told, did he ever talk to women, though he was attended by a woman servant. Nevertheless women are allowed an equal place in Druze ceremonies of worship, though in a segregated chamber.

The origins of the sect make an extraordinary story. They go back to a boy-Caliph of Egypt, al-Hakim. His conduct was so strange that he was taken to be divine by some of his followers, like other descendants of Ali, who married the Prophet's daughter, Fatima. Others considered him insane. To orthodox Sunni Muslims he is a great heretic. He succeeded to the Caliphate in AD 996 at the age of eleven and grew up to be ever more fanatical and puritanical. Though his mother was a Christian, he decreed that Christians should wear distinguishing clothing and display a cross weighing five pounds on a chain from their necks. He demolished Christian churches, including the Church of the Resurrection in Jerusalem. He ordered all vines to be uprooted, to enforce the Koran's prohibition of wine-drinking. He prohibited banquets and music and forbade women to go out in the streets of Cairo. He even forbade his followers to play chess. Two Persians were among the first to proclaim him as the final manifestation of Allah in human form. One of them, al-Darazi, was sent as a missionary to Mount Hermon in Lebanon, where he found a following among the mountain people. They were Shiites who took the name of Druze from al-Darazi. He was killed in battle and was succeeded as the Caliph's right-hand man by another Persian called Hamzah, who was still in Cairo. In 1020, al-Hakim, the Caliph, disappeared on his evening walk to a hill outside Cairo. He is believed to have been murdered, but Hamzah proclaimed he was not dead but immortal, hidden from human view until the time when he would return to claim his faithful people in triumph. He became the 'hidden Imam' – an idea that was already familiar among the Shiite Muslims, who believed that the line of true Imams or Caliphs descended from Ali had ended with just such another disappearance. Letters were written to the Christians of Constantinople and other places inviting them to recognize that God had again appeared in the human form of al-Hakim, the commander of the Believers, and that Hamzah was his Messiah. This apparently met with no response or conversions and it was then announced that 'the door had been closed' and there would be no more recruiting of converts. Henceforward the Druze religion must never be divulged to outsiders, presumably until the second coming of al-

Hakim. At this point, the Druze faith diverged markedly from Islam. Not only did Hamzah substitute himself for Muhammad as the most important messenger of God, he absolved his followers from the five cardinal obligations of Islam – fasting, prayer and pilgrimage to Mecca among them. He announced seven new precepts, first among them absolute truthfulness, and protection and mutual aid between all members of the faith. It is this precept of mutual aid which above all has kept the Druzes together as a compact, united body which has survived as a small minority group unchanged for nearly 1000 years. Among their other mystical beliefs are predestination and the transmigration of souls. The fact that the Druzes believe that, on death, they are immediately reincarnated in a newborn child, has made them fearless warriors with a reputation for defying authority successfully in their mountain fortresses. Quite logically, they erect no gravestones.

The largest influx of the Druzes into the Jebel occurred in the 1860s after they rose against the Maronite Christians in the Lebanon and massacred them in thousands. A French expeditionary force was sent out by a horrified Europe to end this religious civil war and thousands of Druzes fled to Syria and settled in the inhospitable land of the Jebel, where they built their capital, Souwayda. They found there the ruins of an ancient city of the Nabatean kingdom, which flourished in the first century AD and was ruled from Petra, further south. Souwayda is now the chief town of the district but its ancient ruins disappeared almost entirely in its rebuilding by the Druzes. There are just four columns left of the Temple of Dusares, the Nabatean god. The city was renamed Dionysias by the Romans when they annexed the province. A museum preserves the Roman mosaics and such statues of the Nabatean and Roman

period as survive. Up in the hills, about five miles away, stands the Druze village of Qanawat where the pillars of a temple to the Sun God, Helios, stand out above the fields; there is also the remains of a big basilica, for this little place far from the main roads once had its own Christian bishop. But the place for Roman remains on a grand scale is Bosra, which the emperor Trajan conquered

Bosra: the gateway which alone survives from the Nabatean city

in the year AD 106 and made into the capital of his new Provincia Arabia. This comprised the wild lands of the Jebel, the nomadic tribes, and the great wheat-growing plains around Bosra, the Hauran, which became the granary of the empire. Five roads met at Bosra and it lay on the caravan route to the Red Sea and to the Arabian Gulf. It grew to be one of the biggest cities of the empire.

It minted its own coins and introduced a new era of dates, beginning with its foundation as Nova Trajana Bosra in 106. You would hardly believe all this now as you drive into the squat, black, single-storey remnants of the town's outskirts. Here and there a lonely column pokes its head above the humble roofs. It looks as though it has been wrecked in a war and left to improvise

145

some sort of haphazard life in the ruins. All of which adds to the astonishment when you penetrate to the Roman heart of the city where you will find the main colonnaded street, known to Romans as the Decumanus, still bisecting the town from west to east. It stretches – as at Apamea and Palmyra – for over a mile, still paved with the great blocks of basalt that the Romans laid. Trees grow where the colonnades once stood while the barrel sections of the columns lie discarded along the kerb. The long vista is closed by the double arch of the western gate to the city. This is the 'Gate of the Winds', which leads on to Deraa twenty-five miles away, on the borders of Syria and Jordan where the main road south now passes, leaving Bosra isolated. People still live along the length of this street in modest houses raised on the foundations and cellars of the Roman shops and villas. In front of many of them you will see the capitals of the colonnade – Ionic, not Corinthian – put outside like gateposts. The inhabitants sit on them in the evenings to watch the passers-by. For the only traffic on this great thoroughfare today is donkeys or sheep and the colourful figures of the Druzes, the women in sky-blue and maroon gowns, or scarlet and gold, balancing bundles and baskets and cardboard packing cases on their heads. The girl children, often astonishingly blonde, with their hair in coiled plaits, balance tins and mats on theirs while the boys dash along bowling bicycle wheels. At the halfway point of the Decumanus is the crossing where it was bisected by the north-south axis, which the Romans called the *cardo* (all Roman town-plans are the same). The Decumanus has been built up at this point and, from the side, you can see how. Under the cobbles, rows of barrel sections of the colonnade have been used as a foundation for the roadway. Just beside it still stand two upright columns of the temple, complete with a chunk of

elaborately carved cornice. On top of all this someone has stuck the loudspeaker used to call the Muslims to the mosque for prayer. This improvisation is typical of the place. Part of its charm is the way the lordly remnants of Roman rule have been put to homely use. Elsewhere you can see a solitary Corinthian pillar with a dovecote placed on top of it – a very superior address for doves. At the top of the Decumanus stands a triple-arched gateway, the only survival from the Nabatean city that preceded the Roman one and the only Nabatean arch to be found outside Petra. Climb down through it and there is a maze of little dusty streets winding away on the hillside, still lined with tumble-down walls and dwellings of black basalt. Some are now stables, some are deserted, and some have been adapted to form modest houses. You step through a gateway in a wall to find a courtyard with chickens, a vine, a small garden and a Druze family. The man, in pantaloons, may ask you in and offer you small cups of bitter coffee. Their house is constructed against the crumbling black walls and stairways built 1700 years earlier. Inside, the walls are hung with carpets and the only furniture in the little front room is a high ottoman piled with cushions. Not far away, through more deserted, winding alley-ways between abandoned houses, stands an immense basilica, seat of an archbishop when it was built in 512. It was the first to be built with a dome and it inspired Justinian, the emperor of the time, to build the great domes of Santa Sophia in Constantinople. Just down the street is a more modest abandoned church, its wide archway closed by railings, through which you can look at the back wall and its apse, which is letting the daylight through. It is unremarkable as a building but it has a niche in religious history for it was here that the Christian monk, Bahira, was visited by the young Muhammad on his caravan journeys

The Druzes wear long, colourful, embroidered dresses and flowing white veils

A group of Druze children

were it not for its chief glory. At the summit of the hill on which the town is built stands the citadel, a great glowering chunk of black stone erected by the Arabs in the thirteenth century against the crusaders. But having passed through the fortress gates and some massive, dark passageways, you come out through a black archway into an astonishing blaze of sunlight playing on golden brown stone and creamy-pink columns. One is all the more grateful for the warm contrast after the black ruins everywhere else. You are standing in the biggest and best Roman theatre in the Orient and it is in near-perfect order. The Arab fortifications and the barracks which once filled the auditorium protected it inside and out. Now it has been cleared and put back as it was. The stage, the semicircle of the auditorium, the thirty-five rows of seating, the gangways, even the stage boxes stand there trim and serviceable – indeed, it is now in use again for festivals. The Roman architect who constructed it certainly understood acoustics, which you can test for yourself with the help of a friend in the auditorium. A normal speaking voice can be heard perfectly from the stalls to the gallery. From the parapet above, whose top-most ring of Doric columns is almost complete, you can appreciate its size, its steeply raked seats and its perfect eyelines . . . it is as high as the gallery at Drury Lane but the visibility is far better. It is also remarkably comfortable. The stone seats all have over-lapping front edges and those at the back of the 'stalls' have shaped stone backs to lean against. There are even double seats, made for two to share, which no doubt used to cost extra. I have sat in many a less comfortable upholstered seat than these stone ones. It is, undoubtedly, one of the great theatres of the world, as well as one of the biggest. Rome itself would give its eye-teeth to have such a beautiful showpiece still intact.

to Syria with his uncle, and where he may have acquired his knowledge of the Gospels. Because of this belief, Bosra became a stopping place for the pilgrims on their way south from Damascus to Mecca and acquired its ancient mosques and its Arab citadel. One of them, 'the Mosque of the Camel', was alleged to preserve a tile imprinted by the knee of the camel ridden by Muhammad on his visit. Sacred relics to impress the pious are conveniently discovered in all shapes and sizes but this is the first one has heard of a sacred knee-print!

All of these remnants and bygones would hardly persuade travellers to make the journey to such a forlorn and forgotten town,

SYRIA TODAY

S YRIA TOOK its most important leap forward since independence in November 1970, when Lieutenant-General Hafez al Assad seized power and, having been elected president by overwhelming popular vote four months later, inaugurated a programme of stability and ordered progress. Syria badly needed stable government. Since independence and the departure of the French in 1946, it had an unenviable record of almost continuous coups d'état – more than twenty of them in twenty-four years. Under Assad it has found it.

The president is a peasant's son from the sect of Alawites, who inhabit the hilly country around Latakia and form about ten per cent of the Muslim population. He was born in 1930 and became an air force fighter-pilot because, he said, 'I heard French planes were bombing our towns and thought that, if I were a pilot, I could stop them.' He passed out as a pilot and winner of the acrobatic championship and rose to be a general in nine years. When he took over leadership of his country, he was head of the air force and Minister of Defence. His interest in politics began young. At seventeen, he joined the newly formed Syrian Baath Socialist Party along with most of the young intellectuals of his generation. Baath means 'Renaissance' or 'Resurrection' and the party's three basic aims are Arab unity, freedom and socialism. Assad himself has said: 'Our party is not a Marxist party. It is a socialist party with nationalist leanings.' And though Syria is a socialist republic, with state ownership of banks and major enterprises, Assad has not pursued the extreme, doctrinaire socialism and subservience to the Soviet Union of his predecessors. Foreign capital has been not only allowed but encouraged to aid in the economic development the country so badly needed and it has come from Western Europe as well as from the Soviet bloc.

Syria has traditionally been the intellectual leader among Arab states, militant in the cause of Arab unity in face of the threat of Israeli expansionism. It has been host to many of the Palestinian nationalist groups, and leader among the 'steadfast' Arab states who reject Israeli occupation of traditionally Arab lands. This has been especially true since the Egyptian rapprochement and treaty with Israel, which President Assad called 'a stab in the back of the Arab world'. Nevertheless his record has been one of reasonableness on this highly emotive issue. 'The Arabs are one nation,' he declared in an interview with *The Times*, but added, 'We are not fanatics. We do not believe in the purity of the blood as Hitler did. But the bonds that bind us are much stronger than those of people such as in Britain, where you have the English, the Scots, the Welsh and the Irish living within one state . . . Despite continuing hostility of thirty years, we Arabs, as Arab citizens, have no thought of destroying the Jews – of driving them into the sea, as you say. But the Arabs cannot accept continued occupation of their land and the continued displacement of the people of Palestine.' The president has a

The Russian-built turbines in the gleaming marble hall powered by the Euphrates Dam

The oil refinery at Homs helps make Syria self-sufficient

reputation for level-headedness and hard work. Married with five children, he lives austerely – does not smoke or drink – and works until three or four in the morning, expecting his ministers to do likewise. One of his few relaxations is listening to Western classical music, especially Mozart and Wagner. No one can doubt his prime concern is patriotic – to make his country strong after so many years of foreign occupation and instability – or doubt his personal popularity. An overwhelming ninety-seven per cent of the Syrian electorate turned out in 1978 to re-elect him for another seven-year term as President. You will hear tributes to his sagacity, incorruptibility and firm leadership from Syrians in all walks of life. 'With him as our leader we can hold our heads high,' said a Syrian. In spite of sporadic recent outbreaks of terrorism directed against his fellow Alawites, possibly out of religious sectarian rivalry, the President himself commands universal respect in Syria. Under his régime, there have been two five-year plans to develop the economy at a hectic pace up to 1980. Indeed, Syria gives the visitor the impression of a hard-working country making heroic efforts to achieve prosperity in spite of the costly distractions of continual preparedness for war. The three pillars of economic recovery have been energy (provided by the growing Syrian oilfields and the Euphrates Dam); agriculture, aided by massive irrigation schemes; and a fast-developing industry based on home-produced steel and chemicals.

Oil has been drilled since 1971, particularly in the extreme north-east around Qaratchok near the border with Iraq. Annual production, though small by Middle Eastern standards, is eleven million tons and growing, enough to make Syria self-sufficient and leave something for export. There are now two big refineries, at Homs and at Baniyas, on the coast, with the capacity to refine the whole of Syria's output of crude oil, which is connected to them by pipe-line. Some idea of the handicaps under which this has been achieved can be gained from the fact that the 1973 war with Israel left the Homs refinery with half its machinery and two-thirds of its oil tanks destroyed by bombing. They got the installations going again in forty-five days.

Undoubtedly the greatest investment Syria has made in the past decade is the Great Euphrates Dam, the pride of the country. Its function is two-fold – to provide virtually all (ninety-seven per cent) of the country's electricity and to irrigate vast areas of previously arid and unproductive land. The dam took ten years to build and was finished, a year early, in March 1978. It involved the construction of a new lake fifty miles long, named Lake Assad after the president, the removal of 100 riverside villages and the construction of a completely new town, Al-Thaura, to house the 10,000 workers who built and service the dam, its power station and its irrigation channels.

The dam is not just a massive hydro-electric power-house, it is already a tourist attraction as a triumph of modern technology: one and a half billion Syrian pounds-worth of dam. It announces its presence with a low, deeply powerful, grumbling vibration. It sweeps across the clean, empty landscape in a great concrete curve, nearly three miles long, pinning back the bright blue waters of Lake Assad on one side and releasing them, white and foaming, through its eight giant sluices on the other. Standing on the road across the top of it, you feel, rather than hear, the tremble of the turbines beneath. There are eight of them, ranged in the gleaming marble hall of the turbine house. They look like a row of giant red mushrooms standing in this aluminium-walled nave of a cathedral consecrated to the

Where the blue waters of Lake Assad meet the sluices of the Euphrates Dam

gods of electricity and power. On each turbine top (for there is far more hidden, like an iceberg, beneath the floor) are inscribed the words 'Leningrad and Novossibirsk', where the machinery was built. The Russians who installed it have left behind their plaque and a noticeboard of honour, covered with the photographs of the Syrian heroes of labour who built and learnt to operate it under their direction. Each of the 1000 Russian engineers trained their Syrian counterparts and then left them to carry on. There are now not many more than a hundred Russians left. Only one was visible during my visit, supervising the morning shift. Four turbines were humming out of the eight, each with the capacity to produce 142,000 kilowatts. Between them, men on

crossed by a wide road, you pause to watch the great schools of fish that gather and hover not only at the lake's edge but in pools beside the foaming out-flow below the dam. There are carp in this lake which are fished and delivered daily to Damascus. And in the river, there are species which grow into aggressive monsters of 100 kilos. One of the by-products of the dam will be a freshwater fishing industry. A German company is studying what new species to introduce into the lake. The archaeological sites which were submerged as the lake filled up were excavated by foreign missions and their finds are on show in the Aleppo Museum. The fortress of pink stone, Qalaat Jabar, that stands out from the bank like an island with thirty-five turrets is being restored and will be made into a tourist exhibit as a museum and restaurant. A minaret, which stands on a cliff overlooking the lake, was moved and rebuilt there segment by segment. The shores are to be developed for camping and water-skiing and boating holidays.

Below the dam, the great Euphrates now meanders away in many branches separated by rocky islets and mud. The dam has put an end to its spring floods which used to sweep away whole villages. Beside its river-bed, squeaking yellow bulldozers are gouging out irrigation channels. Seven separate regions of the Euphrates basin are being irrigated, their total acreage adding up to 640,000 hectares, more than all the previously irrigated land in Syria put together. Pilot schemes, operated by French, Russian, Romanian and Japanese agriculturalists have produced remarkable yields of wheat, cotton, rice and vegetables, some of them five times what they were before. Al Thaura itself – the name means 'The Revolution' – is a completely new town built in Russian-style apartment blocks on wide boulevards, for a population of 90,000 people. It is not beautiful, nor characterful, but it is clean,

the duty shift sat at tables reading and playing cards. 'We no longer need Russians to put them right – we are all Syrians here now,' explained a foreman. 'They have been running for four years without trouble.' And, listening to the low-pitched throbbing beneath our feet, he added proudly, 'That is the economy of Syria.'

On the long walk across the parapet,

Upended shell-cases grow a few parched flowers on the desolate frontier

The interior of Qunaitra hospital, riddled with Israeli bullets

quiet and free of traffic problems. It is a socialist, utopian city in which all the buildings are state-owned. The pioneers who live there have to endure extreme temperatures – forty-five degrees centigrade in summer, and down to minus seven degrees in the winter. No wonder, I thought, one of the functionaries of the dam has a snow-scene on the wall of his office. Then he amazed me by telling me they had snow in the area during some winters. Much of the newly fertile land on the Euphrates belongs to the state or is worked by co-operatives. Agrarian reform has limited the scope of private farming. Individual holdings may not be more than eight hectares in irrigated areas, thirty hectares in non-irrigated areas with ample rainfall and forty-five hectares in the dryer areas. Agriculture employs half the working population and accounts for a fifth of the country's exports, especially cotton. Meanwhile industry has been expanded greatly, based on Syria's own iron deposits and steel-making plants. Syria now makes its own tractors, refrigerators, washing machines and television sets, among other things, and the annual Damascus International Trade Fair in July attracts 2000 exhibitors and over a million visitors.

The other major investment is in education. The French left Syria with a high illiteracy rate and few schools. Now almost a quarter of the country's eight million people are enrolled in an educational institution. There are forty times as many pupils in secondary schools as in 1946 and the number of students at university now exceeds 65,000, about a third of them women. Damascus University, the oldest and largest, teaches all subjects, including science, in Arabic. Science faculties now take over forty per cent of the students and the engineering faculty of 6000 includes, interestingly, no fewer than 600 women students. University education is free to Syrians and Palestinians but, if the student fails the finals, the tuition fees have to be repaid. The State investment in higher education amounts to £(Syrian)163 per head of the population which, in a hard-pressed economy of which more than a quarter of the budget goes on military defence, is heroic as well as far-sighted. There is thirty months' compulsory military service for all Syria's young men.

The reason for this costly state of preparedness is obvious when you drive south-west from Damascus towards the Israeli border. There lies the town of Qunaitra, captured by the Israelis in the 1967 war and returned under the cease-fire negotiations after the war of 1973. Before it was handed over in 1974, the Israelis evacuated the Arab population of some 37,000 and spent a week methodically destroying it. Everything that could be removed, from windows to electric fittings, was sold to Israeli contractors and the houses and shops were literally pulled apart with tractors and bulldozers. The minaret of the mosque has a shell-hole through it; the Christian church was stripped to the bare walls, the hospital was sprayed with machine-gun bullets, even the graves in the cemetery were broken open and robbed. This scene of wanton devastation – for the town was not a battlefield – has paradoxically turned its forlorn wreckage into a propaganda showpiece, to demonstrate the intransigence of the Israelis. It also demonstrates the ever-present threat on Syria's border. Qunaitra lies half-encircled by Israeli-held hills. From the Golan Heights on Mount Hermon to the ring of foothills cradling the devastated town, Israeli gun emplacements and radio masts overlook every square yard of Syrian soil. Though they gave the town back, in practice they still hold it in their grip. There is little point in rebuilding – for who would live here under the guns of the opposing front line?

Qunaitra : not the result of an earthquake but of Israeli occupation

A poster of President Assad stuck defiantly on the ruins of Qunaitra

The only inhabitants of the town are the UN peace-keeping force, their white trucks whizzing through the empty streets, their blue-capped soldiers drawn from faraway Austria, Poland or Ireland. Their radar antennae monitor both sides of the border for signs of conflict, which, if it came, they would be powerless to prevent. All around stretches a battle-scarred plain, a bleak infer-

tile country good for tanks but for little else. Three frontier posts lie within 200 yards of each other along the road: the Syrian, the UN and the Israeli, each flying their flags. A sentry sits by the barrier on an old car seat with its springs going rusty. Up-ended shell cases grow a few parched flowers outside the guard-hut. One Albertine rose flowers forlornly and pathetically, a

The last frontier post at Qunaitra. The Israeli flag flies just down the road

reminder of how different this bleak corner of the earth could be if men could live at peace. One of the lessons of a visit to Syria is the realization that for 3000 years Arab and Jew, Muslim and Christian have lived in this land side by side in reasonable harmony until our own time – which makes the present armed and embattled stalemate all the more saddening.

The biggest political development affecting Syria for many years has been the rapprochement with its neighbour, Iraq. After many years of bitter quarrelling, it took their common opposition to the Camp David talks between Egypt and Israel to bring them together. In October 1978, the presidents of the two countries met for the first time in five years. President Assad was

Memorial to a Syrian fighter-pilot on the plains below the Golan Heights

greeted in Baghdad with flowers, a salute of guns and a golden key to the city. They signed a charter of mutual co-operation and announced plans of co-ordinating their economies and military forces. The borders and the pipelines between them were re-opened. Indeed, proposals were made and explored that the two countries might be merged into some form of a federal state, with joint ministries for foreign affairs and defence. It is too early to predict what the outcome of this exploration may be, but there can be no doubt that a new understanding between two such powerful Arab neighbours would alter the whole power balance in the Middle East. Syria could only emerge from it economically strengthened.

Tourism came late to Syria. Though archaeologists have always known of its fascination and importance, the layman from Europe has largely passed it by, more from ignorance than for any other reason. In recent years, the Syrian government has begun an ambitious programme of hotel building and resort development to catch up with its neighbours in the eastern Mediterranean and this has now borne fruit in up-to-date accommodation and transport.

But there is an advantage for the visitor in this slower pace of tourist development. While so many countries of the world are becoming almost indistinguishable from one another under the pressure of tourist standardization, Syria has kept itself relatively unchanged and unspoilt. It has not destroyed its past in coming to terms with its present. It treats its thousands of years of history with respect and preserves them. There are few countries where one is more conscious of the continuity with the past, as has been exemplified in this book. And there are few modern and highly civilized countries which still feel to the visitor as authentically different, oriental and mysteriously unique as Syria.